Writing Sentences and Paragraphs

by
Bonnie L. Walker, Ph.D.

AGS®

American Guidance Service, Inc.
4201 Woodland Road
Circle Pines, MN 55014-1796
1-800-328-2560

Introduction

This book is about writing effective sentences and paragraphs. Effective means "producing the desired effect, impressive."

A **sentence** is a group of words that expresses a complete idea. Writers begin with an idea they wish to express to someone else. They use a group of words called a sentence.

A **paragraph** is a group of sentences about a single topic. Often, ideas are too complex to express in one sentence. Writers need to explain their idea with details or examples.

An **essay** or **composition** is a group of paragraphs about a single topic. When an idea is too complex to explain in one paragraph, writers break up the topic into many subtopics.

Sentences, paragraphs, and essays all help writers express their ideas. Writing is *effective* when writers successfully communicate with other people.

No matter what we write, we go through certain steps.

- We think about what we want to say. We organize our thoughts.
- We may do some research. This is called *prewriting*.
- We write down our ideas. This is called the *first draft*.
- We *proofread;* we make changes, or *revise;* and we produce a *final draft*.

Write a short paragraph (about three to five sentences) describing a place you have visited. Use your own paper. Proofread your paragraph. Make changes. Rewrite it on a separate piece of paper.

Printed in the United States of America

ISBN 0–7854–0945–9 (Previously ISBN 0–88671–962–3)

Product Number 90841

Contents

Introduction 2
Unit 1: **Sentences Are Made of Words**
  Lesson 1: Problem Words 5
  Lesson 2: The Exact Meaning: Denotation and Connotation 6
  Lesson 3: Loaded Words and Euphemisms 7
  Lesson 4: Synonyms: Words That Mean the Same 8
  Lesson 5: Antonyms: Words with Opposite Meanings 9
  Lesson 6: Homophones: Words That "Sound" the Same 10
  Lesson 7: Sound-Alike Words 11
  Review: Proofread, Revise, Recopy 12
Unit 2: **The Importance of Spelling**
  Lesson 1: The Sounds of Words 13
  Lesson 2: Identifying Suffixes 14
  Lesson 3: Plural Nouns 15
  Lesson 4: Past Tense of Verbs 16
  Lesson 5: The Final *E* 17
  Lesson 6: Doubling the Final Consonant 18
  Review: Proofread, Revise, Recopy 19
Unit 3: **Sentence Rules**
  Lesson 1: Beginning a Sentence 20
  Lesson 2: Ending a Sentence 21
  Lesson 3: Sentence Fragments 22
  Lesson 4: Run-on Sentences 23
  Lesson 5: Words and Phrases in a Series 24
  Lesson 6: Compound Sentences 25
  Lesson 7: Complex Sentences 26
  Lesson 8: Dialogue: Direct and Indirect Quotations 27
  Review: Proofread, Revise, Recopy 28
  Test: Units 1–3 29
Unit 4: **Writing Correct Sentences**
  Lesson 1: Singular and Plural 30
  Lesson 2: Agreement of Subject and Verb 31
  Lesson 3: Using Pronouns Correctly 32
  Lesson 4: The Case of the Pronoun 33
  Lesson 5: Plurals and Possessives 34
  Lesson 6: Using Verbs Correctly: Verb Tense 35
  Lesson 7: Progressive Tenses 36
  Lesson 8: Conditional Tenses 37
  Lesson 9: Logical Verb Tense 38
  Lesson 10: Comparisons 39
  Lesson 11: Starting a Sentence 40
  Review: Proofread, Revise, Recopy 41
Unit 5: **The Writer's Toolbox**
  Lesson 1: Using a Dictionary 42
  Lesson 2: Dictionary Entries 43
  Lesson 3: The Thesaurus 44
  Lesson 4: Sample Entry 45
  Review: Proofread, Revise, Recopy 46
Unit 6: **Sentences Make Paragraphs**
  Lesson 1: Writing Paragraphs 47
  Lesson 2: Topic Sentences 48
  Lesson 3: Supporting the Main Idea 49
  Lesson 4: Adding Details and Examples 50
  Lesson 5: Conclusions and Summaries 51
  Lesson 6: Weeding Out the Extraneous 52
  Review: Proofread, Revise, and Recopy 53

Unit 7:   **The Art of Paraphrasing**
    Lesson 1: Rewriting   54
    Lesson 2: In Your Own Words   55
    Lesson 3: Spice It Up!   56
    Review: Paraphrasing   57
    Test: Units 4–7   58

Unit 8:   **Writing in Pictures**
    Lesson 1: The Descriptive Approach   59
    Lesson 2: Using Adjectives and Adverbs   60
    Lesson 3: Similes and Metaphors   61
    Lesson 4: Personification   62
    Review: Descriptive Writing   63

Unit 9:   **Expressing Ideas**
    Lesson 1: The Expository Paragraph   64
    Lesson 2: Happiness Is ...: Writing Definitions   65
    Lesson 3: The Book Report   66
    Lesson 4: Movie and TV Reviews   67
    Lesson 5: How To...   68
    Review: Expository Writing   69

Unit 10:   **Improving Your Writing**
    Lesson 1: Say What You Mean   70
    Lesson 2: The Active Voice   71
    Lesson 3: A Strong Beginning   72
    Lesson 4: Expressing Feelings   73
    Review: Proofread, Revise, Recopy   74
    Test: Units 8–10   75

Unit 11:   **Telling a Story**
    Lesson 1: The Narrative Paragraph   76
    Lesson 2: Flashbacks   77
    Lesson 3: It Happened to Me: First Person Narrative   78
    Lesson 4: Direct Quotations   79
    Lesson 5: Indirect Quotations   80
    Lesson 6: Characterization   81
    Lesson 7: Using Your Imagination: Dramatic License   82
    Review: Narrative Writing   83

Unit 12:   **Do You Agree?**
    Lesson 1: Persuasive Writing   84
    Lesson 2: Slogans   85
    Lesson 3: Using Facts to Persuade   86
    Lesson 4: Letter to the Editor   87
    Review: Persuasive Writing   88

Unit 13:   **Writing Letters**
    Lesson 1: The Letter Format   89
    Lesson 2: Personal Letters   90
    Lesson 3: Business Letters   91
    Lesson 4: Addressing Envelopes   92
    Review: Letter Writing   93
    Test: Units 11–13   94

End-of-Book Test   95

Problem Words

Problem Words

When we write, we have problems with certain words.

➤ **Homophones** are words that sound alike but have different meanings. We pronounce them the same, but we spell them differently.

  here—hear

➤ **Synonyms** are words that have almost the same meanings.

  breathtaking—thrilling

➤ **Antonyms** are words that have opposite meanings.

  tiny—huge

➤ **Sound-alike words** may be especially confusing. They are words that may have similar meanings and spellings.

  probably—probable

A Match the words below with their meanings.

1. homophones

2. synonyms

3. antonyms

4. sound-alike words

a. Words that may have a similar spelling or sound

b. Words that sound the same but have different spellings and meanings

c. Words that have almost the same meaning

d. Words that have opposite meanings

B Study each pair of words. Tell whether the words in each pair are homophones, synonyms, antonyms, or sound-alike words. Write your answer on the line.

1. own, possess _____

2. accept, except _____

3. break, brake _____

4. give, take _____

5. their, there _____

6. tall, short _____

7. advice, advise _____

8. answer, respond _____

The Exact Meaning: Denotation and Connotation   Lesson 2

➤ **Denotation** is the exact dictionary meaning of a word. *Denote* means "express ideas briefly or generally."

➤ **Connotation** is emotional meaning suggested by or associated with a word. *Connote* means "suggest or convey a word's associations."

When we write, it is important to understand the emotional impact that certain words have. For example, study the two sentences below. Both *inexpensive* and *cheap* mean "low in price." How are their *connotations* different?

Judi's sweater is *inexpensive*
Judi's sweater is *cheap*.

Inexpensive means "low in cost." It also means "a good value for the money."

Cheap means "low in cost." It also means "of little value" and "easily gotten."

For each expression in bold, substitute another expression that has a stronger emotional meaning.

1. "I am going **to my house** now," said Javier.   _____

2. Kenny is **well-known** in our neighborhood.   _____

3. Sylvia is a **very good** student.   _____

4. Mrs. Harris is a **nice** person.   _____

5. The Rocky Mountains are **beautiful** to see.   _____

6. The fullback on our football team is **strong**.   _____

7. There was **a lot of food** on the table.   _____

8. Homemade ice cream tastes **good.**   _____

9. We had **fine** weather for the picnic.   _____

10. Ellen put a **pretty** quilt on the bed.   _____

11. The clown held a **big** bunch of balloons.   _____

12. It's a **long** journey to the top of Mount Everest.   _____

13. The thunder was **loud.**   _____

14. Too much sun is **bad for you.**   _____

15. Mr. Hardy gave us the **hard** problems last.   _____

Loaded Words and Euphemisms

➤ **Loaded words** are words with strong emotional impact. They are often used in advertising. They are also used in speeches and arguments when the speaker's intention is to stir an audience into action.

A Think of eight examples of words that stir up favorable reactions.
Examples: *home, liberty, freedom,* and *friendship.*

1. _____   5. _____
2. _____   6. _____
3. _____   7. _____
4. _____   8. _____

B Think of eight examples of words that stir up unfavorable reactions.
Examples: *out-dated, unhealthy,* and *nag.*

1. _____   5. _____
2. _____   6. _____
3. _____   7. _____
4. _____   8. _____

➤ A **euphemism** is the use of a less direct word or phrase for one considered impolite or abrupt. It is a word or group of words that does not have much emotional weight. We choose these words to be polite.

Direct word: John is *very old.*

Euphemism: John is *a senior citizen.*

C For each set of sentences, choose the one that contains the euphemism. Write the letter of your answer on each line.

_____ 1. **a.** Carol is rude.   **b.** Carol treats others with disrespect.

_____ 2. **a.** Twyla is not very neat.   **b.** Twyla is messy.

_____ 3. **a.** Jack is with his friends.   **b.** Jack is with his gang.

_____ 4. **a.** Clarisse steals.   **b.** Clarisse borrows without asking.

Synonyms: Words That Mean the Same

➤ A **synonym** is a word that has almost the same meaning as another word. We can find synonyms in the dictionary or in a special book called a *thesaurus*. One word may have many synonyms. Look at the example in the box.

> **Ship:** vessel, boat, craft, sail, liner, yacht, steamer, cutter

A Match the synonyms. Write the letter of your answer on each line.

_____	1. polite	a. picture
_____	2. delicious	b. help
_____	3. quiet	c. want
_____	4. small	d. agreeable
_____	5. tool	e. proper
_____	6. pleasant	f. tasty
_____	7. assist	g. tiny
_____	8. desire	h. utensil
_____	9. correct	i. courteous
_____	10. photograph	j. silent

B Some words, such as *tall* and *high,* have meanings that are almost alike, but we use the words differently. Write the words to complete the sentences.

Example: The basketball player is **tall**. The Rocky Mountains are **high**.

1. I am wearing a _____ shirt. Are these vegetables _____ ? (new, fresh)

2. Cooks work with kitchen _____. Plumbers use _____ to tighten the pipes. (tools, utensils)

3. Here is a _____ of the puzzle. Is this a _____ of your kit? (part, piece)

4. Please _____ your brother for dinner. Do not _____ at him. (shout, call)

5. Did you _____ the letter? Please _____ the door. (seal, shut)

6. The earth _____ around the sun. The dancer _____ and leaps to the music. (turns, revolves)

Antonyms: Words with Opposite Meanings

➤ An **antonym** is a word that means the opposite of another word.

hot   cold   sweet   sour

Heads   **Tails**

Some antonyms have the prefix *un-* or *in-*.

necessary   unnecessary   exact   inexact

 Fill in each blank with a word that means the opposite of the word in parentheses. Use a dictionary if necessary. You may use words from the word box or words of your own.

formal	frigid	helpful	often	smile
friends	frugal	liberty	similar	wild

1. Marietta _____ practiced her free-throw shots. (seldom)

2. In the morning, the baby wakes up with a _____. (frown)

3. "Give me _____ or give me death," said Patrick Henry. (dependence)

4. The winter day was _____. (hot)

5. Mrs. Carson was known for being _____. (wasteful)

6. Terell and Rita have been _____ for years. (enemies)

7. The two songs had very _____ beats. (different)

8. The _____ horses live in the canyon. (tame)

9. The graduation was a _____ occasion. (casual)

10. My counselor gave me some _____ advice about classes to take. (useless)

 Learning new words can be fun. Look through a dictionary and choose ten words that you do not know. Write them down. Write down their meanings. Use them in a sentence. Look and listen for those words in your everyday life—in the newspaper or on television.

Homophones: Words That "Sound" the Same

➤ A **homophone** is a word that sounds the same as another word. The meaning of the two words are different. People often make errors with homophones.

Some of the Most Commonly Mixed-up Homophones

There—adverb of location	Jakob lives over **there.**
Their—possessive pronoun	**Their** house is on the corner.
They're—contraction	**They're** expected to arrive soon.
Too—adverb of degree	That shirt is **too** expensive.
To—preposition	Tina walked **to** school today.
Two—a number	Masumi bought **two** tires for her bicycle.
Hear—to receive sound through the ears	Did you **hear** the thunder?
Here—this place	**Here** is where I live.

A Fill in each blank with the correct word.

1. Did you look over _____ for your keys? (there, their, they're)

2. Have you been invited to _____ house? (there, their, they're)

3. _____ repairing the roof of the garage. (There, Their, They're)

4. Last week was _____ cold for swimming. (too, to, two)

5. We went _____ the park for a picnic. (too, to, two)

6. Denise's sister is _____ years old today. (too, to, two)

7. Please put the chair _____ next to the table. (hear, here)

8. Did you _____ the birds chirping this morning? (hear, here)

B Look up the following pairs of words in a dictionary. Then use each one correctly in a sentence.

1. a. passed _____

   b. past _____

2. a. through _____

   b. threw _____

3. a. your _____

   b. you're _____

4. a. buy _____

   b. by _____

5. a. whether _____

   b. weather _____

Sound-Alike Words

➤**Sound-alike words** have similar meanings and spellings.

county—a subdivision of a state	Fred lives in Allen **County**.
country—a nation or a rural area	My **country** is the United States.
probable—(adjective) likely to happen or to be true	Rain today is **probable**.
probably—(adverb) likely to happen or to be true	It will **probably** rain today.
then—at that time; next in time	He fed the dog and **then** gave it water.
than—a word used to introduce a comparison	I'd rather have milk **than** water.
quiet—still; calm; motionless	The house is very **quiet** at night.
quite—completely; actually	I am not **quite** finished with my report.

A Fill in each blank with the correct word. Choose your answer from the words in parentheses.

1. Are you _____ sure this is the right exit? (quite, quiet)

2. The night was so _____ you could hear the stars twinkling. (quite, quiet)

3. The _____ path of the storm is from northwest to southeast. (probable, probably)

4. Since traffic is heavy, Niko will _____ be late. (probable, probably)

5. Elaine is taller _____ her brother Jackson. (then, than)

6. We had a snack and _____ watched the movie. (then, than)

7. She lives in Montgomery _____ in Maryland. (County, Country)

8. There are 12 _____ in South America. (counties, countries)

B Use each pair of words in a sentence.

1. a. **advice**—*noun,* an opinion you give to another person about what to do

   b. **advise**—*verb,* to give someone your opinion about what they could do

   a. _____

   b. _____

2. a. **formerly**—*adverb,* in earlier times; in the past

   b. **formally**—*adverb,* according to the rules; the opposite of *casually*

   a. _____

   b. _____

Review: Proofread, Revise, Recopy

An important part of the writing process is revising your work. Here are three words to know.

➤ *Proofread* means "to look for mistakes."
➤ *Revise* means "to change."
➤ *Recopy* means "to copy over."

A Cross out the words in bold print. Replace them with synonyms. Write your answers above the crossed-out words. Use the dictionary if necessary.

A Trip to Ireland

Mr. and Mrs. Garman took a **trip** to Ireland last month. They **visited** Dublin, Cork, Limerick, and Galway and many other **places.** They went to County Waterford, which is **well-known** for the cut glass produced there. They **really** liked the Lakes of Killarney in County Kerry. They said that the green countryside is **beautiful.** When they **came back** home, they showed their friends their **pictures.** The Garmans said that Ireland is a **great** vacation spot. They **want to** return there someday.

B Cross out each word in bold print. Replace each word with an antonym. Write your answer above each word. Use the dictionary if necessary.

1. The new puppy was **noisy** all night.
2. Howard's work was **incomplete.**
3. The airplane will **arrive** at noon.
4. Anna Marie **scolded** the puppy.
5. The story is about a **cruel** ruler.

C Carefully check each word in bold print. Cross out each incorrect word. Write the correct word above it.

Evenings in the mountains are usually **quite.** That fact is **probable** true in many parts of the **country.** In the summer, the **whether** is normally **quite** pleasant **hear.** So **by** yourself a tent, and plan to camp out. **Your** going to love **your** vacation in the great outdoors!

The Sounds of Words

Spelling is always important. You cannot write effective sentences and paragraphs unless your spelling is "letter perfect."

One of the most important aids to spelling is "sounding out" a word. It is important to pronounce every syllable.

➤ A **syllable** is a part of a word. Each syllable has a vowel sound. The vowels are *a, e, i, o, u* and sometimes *y* and *w.* All the other letters are consonants.

➤ The final *e* usually does not have a vowel sound. For example, the word *rose* has only one syllable.

➤ Two vowels side-by-side may form a **vowel blend**. A vowel blend makes only one vowel sound, and so there is only one syllable. For example, the word *soup* has only one syllable.

Examples: house   per/fect   com/po/si/tion
                 (one syllable) (two syllables) (four syllables)

 Write the correct answer on each line.

	How many vowels do you see?	How many vowels do you hear?	Write the word in syllables.
1. jump			
2. record			
3. wonderful			
4. velvet			
5. vacation			
6. terrific			
7. magazine			
8. health			
9. thirsty			
10. know			
11. bicycle			
12. about			
13. idea			
14. under			
15. lion			

Identifying Suffixes

➤ A **suffix** is an ending added to a word. The main part of the word is called the **base word**. A suffix changes the meaning of a word—sometimes a little, sometimes a lot.

Some of the most common suffixes are those we add to verbs: *-s, -ing,* and *-ed.*

Base Words	Base Words with Suffixes
run sing walk	run**s** sing**ing** walk**ed**

Other common suffixes are those we add to nouns to make them plural: *-s* and *-es.*

Base Words	Base Words with Suffixes
cup dish	cup**s** dish**es**

We also add suffixes to change the parts of speech.

Base Words	Base Words with Suffixes
nation teach loyal	nation**al** teach**er** loyal**ty**
(noun) (verb) (adjective)	(adjective) (noun) (noun)

A Circle the suffix on each of the following words.

Verbs	Plural Nouns	Other Words
1. likes	6. books	11. laughable
2. worked	7. presses	12. foolish
3. dancing	8. careful	13. nameless
4. jumped	9. boxes	14. greatness
5. sings	10. slowly	15. excitement

B Add a suffix to each of the words below. Write the new word. Add *-er, -or, -ed, -ing, -s,* or *-es.* Check the new words in a dictionary.

1. sail	_____	6. wait	_____
2. teach	_____	7. stamp	_____
3. machine	_____	8. direct	_____
4. act	_____	9. pass	_____
5. egg	_____	10. sleep	_____

Plural Nouns

➤ **Singular** means "one." **Plural** means "more than one."
   tree   **trees**

Rules for Making Words Plural

Rule 1: We usually change nouns from singular to plural by adding -*s*.
   cup   cup**s**   book   book**s**

Rule 2: To make nouns that end in *sh, ch, x,* and *z* plural, add -*es*.
   box   box**es**   ditch   ditch**es**

Rule 3: When a noun ends in *y* and the letter before the *y* is a consonant, change the *y* to *i* and add -*es*.
   story   stor**ies**   copy   cop**ies**

Rule 4: When a nouns ends in *y* and the letter before the *y* is a vowel, just add -*s*.
   a boy   boy**s**

Rule 5: When a noun ends in *f* or *fe,* usually you change the *f* or *fe* to *v* and add -*es*.
   calf   cal**ves**   life   li**ves**

Rule 6: A few nouns are *very irregular*. They change the vowel inside the word instead of adding a suffix, or they add a suffix that does not contain an -*s*.
   foot   f**ee**t   child   child**ren**

Rule 7: In a very few cases, the singular and plural forms of the noun are the same. You do not add an -*s* or make any other changes.
   one deer   many deer

■ Change each of the following singular nouns to plural. Check a dictionary if necessary.

1. tooth   _____   8. gentleman   _____
2. baby   _____   9. leaf   _____
3. wish   _____   10. church   _____
4. tax   _____   11. chimney   _____
5. lady   _____   12. charity   _____
6. shelf   _____   13. bench   _____
7. berry   _____   14. donkey   _____

**U
N
I
T

2**

A careful writer pays special attention to verbs and makes sure they are correct.

➤ The most common way that we make verbs past tense is by adding the suffix *-ed.* Other verbs are called *irregular.* They must be learned individually.

Examples:	**Present**	**Past**	**Present**	**Past**
	I run	I ran	I go	I went
	I am	I was	I catch	I caught

A Proofread the following paragraph. Check the verbs carefully. Cross out any errors. Make corrections. Use a dictionary if necessary.

The Swimming Meet

After Randy **learned** to swim, he **joined** the swim team. He **swimmed** in three events. At his first meet, Randy **losed** every race. He **feeled** awful, but he **decided** to try again. Every morning Randy **practiced.** He **swimmed** many laps. He **enjoyd** swimming. At the second meet, Randy **winned** one race. He **was** very happy, but it **was** not enough. He **wantd** to win first place in every event. Finally, the last meet of the year **arrived.** Randy **wantd** to win. He had **worked** hard and now **was** his chance. That night Randy **taked** home three blue ribbons. His dream had **come** true.

B Fill in each blank with the past tense of the verb in parentheses. Check the dictionary if necessary.

1. Stacy _____ about becoming a lawyer. (think)

2. "I already _____ the dog," said Jason. (feed)

3. Luisa _____ for school an hour ago. (leave)

4. "Who _____ the leftovers?" asked Gary. (eat)

5. Ms. Esther _____ all of her students' papers. (correct)

6. She _____ the drama course last year. (teach)

The Final *E*

Some writers have trouble adding suffixes to words that end in *e*. The final *e* is usually silent. When a word ends in *e* and you want to add a suffix, you must decide whether to keep the *e* or drop it. Here are two rules to learn.

Rule 1: When adding a suffix to words that end with an *e*, keep the *e* when the suffix begins with a consonant.
lone + ly = lonely   hope + less = hopeless

Rule 2: When adding a suffix to words that end with an *e*, drop the *e* when the suffix begins with a vowel.
love + ing = loving   surprise + ed = surprised

A Write each word with its ending. Do your work carefully.

1. bake + ing _____

2. love + able _____

3. receive + ed _____

4. care + less _____

5. hope + ed _____

6. arrive + ed _____

7. peace + ful _____

8. choose + ing _____

9. invite + ing _____

10. excite + ment _____

B Add *-ing* to each verb. Write the new word.

1. ache _____

2. hope _____

3. wait _____

4. bite _____

5. arrive _____

6. age _____

7. chase _____

8. dive _____

9. advise _____

10. jump _____

C Read the paragraph. Correct any mistakes you find.

The Garden

Geanine and Don decideed to plant a garden. Chooseing the right seed had been very important. They looked at the back of the seed packages to make sure they made the right choices. They were very exciteed about the growing young plants. Geanine and Don enjoyed working in the garden. Geanine was careful to give the plants plenty of water. Don spent many houres weeding the garden. Finally, the floweres bloomed. There were daisyes, marigolds, and zinnias. They were lovly.

Doubling the Final Consonant

Sometimes we double the final consonant of a word before we add an ending. Sometimes the final consonant is *not* doubled. Here are two spelling rules.

Rule 1: When a one-syllable word ends in a single consonant and there is one vowel before the consonant, double the consonant before adding an ending that begins with a vowel.

bat + er = batter

Bat has one syllable. *Bat* ends with the single consonant *t*. The ending *-er* begins with a vowel. You double the final consonant before adding the ending.

Rule 2: When a two-syllable word is accented on the second syllable and it ends in a single consonant preceded by a single vowel, double the consonant before adding an ending that begins with a vowel.

begin + er = beginner

Begin has two syllables. The accent is on the second syllable. *Begin* ends with the single consonant *n*. The ending *-er* begins with a vowel. You double the final consonant before adding the ending.

A Say each word aloud. Draw a line between the two syllables. Circle the words that are accented on the second syllable.

1. signal	3. pilot	5. forgot	7. travel	9. wagon
2. number	4. color	6. open	8. control	10. patrol

B Write each word with its ending. Double the final consonant where necessary. Write the new word in the space.

1. forget + ing _____

2. plan + ing _____

3. jump + ed _____

4. travel + ing _____

5. offer + ing _____

6. color + ful _____

7. differ + ence _____

8. ship + ing _____

9. begin + ing _____

10. regret + able _____

Review: Proofread, Revise, Recopy

■ Follow the directions.

- Proofread the paragraph carefully.
- Correct any mistakes you find. Then recopy the paragraph with your changes.
- Check closely for the following errors:

    Suffixes   Past tense of verbs

The Heat Wave

We haved a heat wave last August. For two weekes in a row, the temperature soarred into the ninetys. Unbelieveably, it even reached 101 degrees. We called these hotest daies of last August "the dog dayes." The air was so still that the leafs did not move. Early in the morning, you heared the birds singging, but by the middle of the morning the livly chirping stoped. Everyone waited for a break in the weather. Finally, the wind beginned to pick up, and the air pressure droped. Relief was on the way.

_____

_____

_____

_____

_____

_____

_____

_____

_____

_____

_____

_____

_____

_____

Beginning a Sentence

Always capitalize the first word in a sentence. A capital letter signals that the sentence has begun. However, capital letters do not always signal the beginning of a sentence. Proper nouns, proper adjectives, and the pronoun *I* are also capitalized.

The end of a sentence always has a period, a question mark, or an exclamation point. Sentences *never* end with a comma.

A Follow the directions.

- Find the beginning and end of each sentence in the paragraph.
- Number each sentence.
- Capitalize the first word of each sentence.
- Recopy each sentence in the space below.

jasper, Melissa's pony, seemed very restless. perhaps Jasper knew that today was the day of the horse show. all week Melissa had been working extra hard. it was her job to brush and groom Jasper. practicing special routines, she also rode him every day. would they win a ribbon? melissa hoped so.

1. _____
2. _____
3. _____
4. _____
5. _____
6. _____
7. _____

B Identify the proper nouns or adjectives and the word *I* in these phrases. Draw three short lines under each letter that should be capitalized.

1. my niece cara
2. the city of san antonio
3. the american dream
4. down the mississippi river

5. my niece and i
6. in the state of texas
7. in the french province
8. over the rocky mountains

Ending a Sentence

Always use an **end mark** at the end of your sentences. There are three end marks: a period, a question mark, and an exclamation point.

There are four types of sentences in English, according to purpose.

- **Statements** end with periods.
- **Commands** or requests end with periods.
- **Questions** end with question marks.
- **Exclamatory sentences** end with exclamation points.

Ann lives in that house.
Please attend the meeting.
Where is the exit?
Oh no, the dog is lost!

A Identify each of the following sentences. Add the proper end mark. Write the type of sentence on each line.

_____ 1. Where is Kenji today

_____ 2. He is at the golf course again

_____ 3. My, that's all he ever does

_____ 4. Don't you like to play golf

_____ 5. Yes, I most certainly do

_____ 6. When do you usually play

_____ 7. Most often, I play on Sunday mornings

_____ 8. Please call me the next time you want to play

B Find the mistakes and write the corrections.

- Capitalize the first word of each sentence
- Add an end mark at the end of each.
- **Hint:** There are 9 sentences in all.

my first day on the golf course was very upsetting have you ever heard

of something called *par* it seems that some people decided how many

times you should hit the ball on each hole that is called par if you hit it in

the hole in one less shot than par, you get a birdie if it takes you one extra

shot, you get a bogey well, I didn't get a single par in fact, I didn't even

get a bogey someone should invent a word for five over par

Sentence Fragments

A group of words do not a sentence make. A fragment is a piece of something.

A sentence expresses a complete idea. It can stand alone. A **sentence fragment** is only a part of a sentence. It cannot stand alone.

Examples: **In the winter**

(This is a prepositional phrase. It is not a sentence.)

Examples: **Because we need practice,**

(This is an introductory adverbial clause. It tells us why something happened.)

A Each item below has a sentence fragment. Rewrite the item so that you have one complete sentence.

1. Wanting to have some place to sell our lemonade. We set up a stand.

_____

2. The dog is barking. At the person who came to the door.

_____

3. Because it has been so hot. We left the city and went to the shore.

_____

4. Karol explained to us. How he could repair the roof of the beach house.

_____

5. Every day when it is early in the morning. I walk to town to get the paper.

_____

B Read each group of words carefully. Decide whether it is a sentence or a fragment. Write *Sentence* or *Fragment* on each line.

_____   1. The old school on the corner over there.

_____   2. It was built in 1895.

_____   3. As a historical landmark in our town.

_____   4. It is a popular site with visitors.

_____   5. Who come here just to visit this historic building.

Run-On Sentences

Run-on sentences are two or more sentences run together without proper punctuation. Sometimes they are connected with *and, or,* and *but.*

Run on: We hiked in the forest, we saw deer, bear, and bison as we hiked.

Correct: We hiked in the forest. **W**e saw deer, bear, and bison as we hiked.

Run on: We crossed the fields but we could not walk through the forest and then we climbed the butte.

Correct: We crossed the fields, but we could not walk through the forest. Then we climbed the butte.

A Follow the directions.

- Cross out all of the *ands, ors,* and *buts* in the example below.
- Rewrite the paragraph in the space.
- Put an end mark at the end of each sentence.
- Capitalize the first word of each new sentence.
- **Hint:** You should have five sentences when you are finished.

The book I read was very good but it made me cry and it was about a horse named Black Beauty and its author was Anna Sewell and I liked it a lot.

_____

_____

_____

_____

_____

Rule to Remember: You cannot use a comma to end a sentence.

B Follow the directions.

- Find the end of each sentence in the example below.
- Put an end mark at the end of each sentence.
- Capitalize the first word of each sentence.
- Use a comma between two clauses and words such as *and, or,* and *but.*
- Rewrite the paragraph on your own paper. You should have five or six sentences when you are finished.

I saw a good movie the other night, we got it at the video store but it was an old movie its name was <u>The Greatest Show on Earth</u> it was about a circus, since it was so good, I'd like to see it again.

Words and Phrases in a Series

Use a comma to separate more than two words or phrases in a series. Place the comma after every item in the series except the last one. Also, use a conjunction such as *and, but,* or *or.*

Effective writers often use **compounds**. A compound is two or more words or phrases in a series. We use a conjunction such as *and* to connect items in a series.

Words in a series

Julie and Harriet are at the movies now.   (Commas are *not* needed.)

Mac, Tory, and Pascal are three of my best friends.   (Commas are needed.)

Phrases in a series

Silvia lives down the street and around the corner.

We got up in the morning, brushed our teeth, and dressed for work.

Rule to Remember: Use a comma to separate three or more items in a series.

A Add commas to each sentence where they are needed. Rewrite the sentence in the space provided.

1. For the party, we bought cola root beer and orange drink.

   _____

2. Howard likes to walk through the woods on mountain trails and on the beach.

   _____

3. Do you prefer a baked potato or rice?

   _____

4. We exercised all morning took classes all afternoon and rested in the evening.

   _____

   _____

B Combine all of the sentences in each list by using a conjunction and commas. Change the verb to agree with a plural subject when necessary.

1. Soccer is fun. Basketball is fun. Swimming is fun.

   _____

2. Mary likes to read. Mary likes to walk. Mary likes to travel.

   _____

3. Mother said she needed bread. She needs milk. She needs vegetables.

   _____

Compound Sentences

A **compound sentence** is two or more "related" sentences joined together with a conjunction. The most common conjunctions are *and, or,* and *but.*

Rule 1: Connect only related ideas.

Right: Buy a house at the beach, **and** you'll suddenly have more friends than you realized.

Wrong: Jack works in the book store, and I used to know him in high school.

Rule 2: Use a comma before the conjunction when you combine two or more sentences.

Right: Cathy went to London, and she visited many historical sites.

Wrong: Sylvia studied very hard for her history test and she got a good grade.

Rule 3: Use *but* to join contrasting ideas.

Right: Donna enjoys playing basketball, **but** she doesn't like cooking.

Wrong: Carrie is twenty-two, but Soren is twenty-two also.

A Combine each pair of sentences below into *one* compound sentence. Add a conjunction and the correct punctuation mark. Write the new sentence in the space provided.

1. Maurice lives in Florida. Allyson lives in Minnesota.

_____

2. My mother's birthday is in August. My father's birthday is in November.

_____

3. You can find Dad in the kitchen. You can find him in the garage.

_____

4. Tennis is played on one kind of court. Basketball is played on another.

_____

B Complete each sentence with either *but* or *and.*

1. Sally likes coffee, _____she does not like tea.

2. As for me, I like coffee, _____I like tea exactly the same.

3. Usually Maura takes a walk, _____ today is too hot for walking.

4. Nancy planned to go swimming, _____it is raining today.

Complex Sentences

Writers often want to express complex ideas; therefore, they need complex sentences.

A **clause** is a group of words with a subject and verb. There are two kinds of clauses: *independent clauses* (clauses that could stand alone as sentences) and *dependent clauses* (clauses that cannot stand alone as sentences).

Independent clause: Marty teaches a computer class.
Dependent clause: Because he enjoys it.

A Identify each group of words as an *Independent* or a *Dependent* clause.

_____   1. Because he was late.

_____   2. John missed the bus.

_____   3. Next time he will get up on time.

Adverb Clause: *When you have the flu*, you should drink lots of fluids.
Noun Clause: I know *what you mean.*
Adjective Clause: There is the girl *whom I met at the pool.*

An *adverb clause* answers the questions when, where, why, or how. A *noun clause* is used just like a noun. In the example above, it is used as a direct object. An *adjective clause* modifies a noun or pronoun. In the example, it describes the girl. It tells us "Which one."

Rule to Remember: Separate an introductory adverbial clause from the independent clause with a comma. Notice the pause at the comma.

Right: *If you are hungry*, I will fix dinner.   (Needs a comma.)
Right: I will fix dinner *if you are hungry.* (Does not need a comma.)

B Underline the dependent clause in each sentence below. Add a comma (pause) to the sentence if necessary.

1. You may invite whomever you want.

2. The boy who sits in the last row rides on my bus.

3. Because Willis wants to be on the honor roll he studies very hard.

4. The game was called off when the thunderstorm began.

Dialogue: Direct and Indirect Quotations

Writers often use dialogue in their writing. **Dialogue** is conversation. Dialogue repeats exactly what someone said.

"Wherever have you been?" asked Jean.

Rule to Remember: Put quotation marks before and after the words someone said. Separate the quotation from the rest of the sentence with a comma or an end mark.

"How many people are still in line?" asked Marisa.

Jeremy replied, "I don't know because most of them are noisy."

A Punctuate these sentences that contain direct quotations.

1. Roland eagerly asked, Will I be able to have the car, Dad?

2. Where's my dictionary? Mildred asked her brother.

3. It is match point, the tennis announcer said.

4. Alisa asked Do you think my computer can be fixed?

5. Wow! This must be the hottest day of the year Sally sighed.

An indirect quotation does not use quotation marks. An *indirect quotation* describes a conversation rather than quotes it exactly.

Indirect Quotation: Last night my mother exclaimed that she had gotten a promotion. I told her how pleased I was for her.

Direct Quotation: "I got a promotion!" my mother exclaimed last night. "I am very pleased for you," I replied.

Rule to Remember: Ordinarily, we start a new paragraph each time a new person speaks. Each speaker's quotation is in a separate paragraph.

B Change each indirect quotation to a direct quotation. Write the direct quotations on the lines below. Remember to start each speaker's words in a new paragraph.

1. Paul told us to meet him at the restaurant at six o'clock.

2. Mary said that she would be there at five.

3. Tony asked if I could drive him to the restaurant.

_____

_____

_____

R
E
V
I
E
W

Follow the directions.

- Proofread the following paragraph carefully.
- Correct any mistakes you find.
- Then recopy the paragraph with your changes.
- **Hint:** Watch out for sentence fragments, run-on sentences, and sentence punctuation. The paragraph contains at least one direct quotation.

Romeo and Juliet

Romeo and Juliet is a play by William Shakespeare and students usually read it in high school? it is a story. about young people who fall in love. They want to get married but the problem is that their families hated each other and Romeo got into a fight with Juliet's cousin and killed him, there was no hope for their love. The play ends in tragedy and people have loved this sad story for hundred of years. Do you know these famous words spoken by Juliet. She said, What's in a name? A rose by any other name would smell as sweet. Oh, Romeo, deny thy name!

_____

_____

_____

_____

_____

_____

_____

_____

_____

_____

_____

_____

_____

_____

_____

Units 1-3 Test

A Write the letter of the response that best completes the sentence on the line.

_____ 1. The words *dear* and *deer* are

         a. synonyms.   **b.** antonyms.   **c.** homophones.   **d.** sound-alike words.

_____ 2. The words *lost* and *found* are

         a. synonyms.   **b.** antonyms.   **c.** homophones.   **d.** sound-alike words.

_____ 3. The words *work* and *labor* are

         a. synonyms.   **b.** antonyms.   **c.** homophones.   **d.** sound-alike words.

B Write your answer on the line.

1. Write the plural of the word *wish.* _____

2. Add the suffix *-ful* to the word *hope.* _____

3. Add the suffix *-est* to the word *hot.* _____

4. Write the plural of the word *country.* _____

5. Add the suffix *-ing* to the word *leave.* _____

6. Write the past tense of the word *go.* _____

7. Write the plural of the word *half.* _____

C Use proofreading marks to add punctuation, delete conjunctions, and capitalize letters in these sentences. Included are run-on sentences, sentence fragments, and errors in punctuation for series, compound and complex sentences, and dialogue.

    I can't believe it, the Chicago Bulls lost the fourth and fifth games of the final playoffs to the Seattle Sonics in June 1996 and they were predicted to win but they did not win. Although the Bulls' star players including Michael Jordan Scottie Pippen Toni Kukoc and Dennis Rodman played. the Bulls were defeated in these games. They did not realize the thrill of victory and they did not win their fourth national championship until Sunday, June 16, 1996. Despite the fact that they worried us. I have to tell the Bulls "we knew you could do it. Congratulations!

Singular and Plural

Singular means "one"; **plural** means "more than one." Only nouns and pronouns can be singular or plural. You can usually recognize a plural noun by its suffix (*-s* or *-es*). Sometimes you need to pay attention to the context. For example, in the sentence below, you know that the word deer is plural even though it doesn't end with an s.

> Five **deer** came to the edge of the woods.

You must memorize the singular and plural forms of pronouns.

A Identify each pronoun as *Singular* or *Plural*

1. he _____
2. they _____
3. our _____
4. I _____
5. us _____

6. she _____
7. we _____
8. them _____
9. it _____
10. her _____

B Identify each word in bold as *Singular* or *Plural*.

1. three **moose** _____
2. **I** am hungry. _____
3. Where are **they**? _____
4. the **elves** _____
5. **His** doctor _____

6. "Joe, **you** are late." _____
7. The **dogs** are barking. _____
8. **my** family _____
9. **Children** play there. _____
10. the salty **crackers** _____

C Change the plurals in bold print into plural pronouns. Write the pronouns in the space provided.

1. The clouds were dark, and **the clouds** were gray. _____

2. **Maurice and I** raced home. _____

3. **Raindrops** began falling. _____

4. I had books, so I covered my head with **my books.** _____

5. It began to pour on **Maurice and me.** _____

6. **He and I** ran into the house. _____

7. Our shoes were wet, so we took **our shoes** off. _____

8. I laughed, "**You and I** won't need a shower tonight!" _____

Agreement of Subject and Verb

Every sentence has a subject and a verb. They must agree in number. A singular subject needs a singular verb form. A plural subject needs a plural verb form.

Subject   **Verb**

The **child wants** that toy.

Subject   **Verb**

The **children want** that toy.

Rules: When the subject is singular, the present tense verb usually ends in *-s* or *-es.*

When the subject is the singular pronoun *you* or *I,* the present tense verb has no ending.

When the subject is plural, the present tense verb has no ending.

A The subject of each sentence is in bold print. Decide if it is singular or plural. Choose the correct form of the verb. Write it on the line.

1. Every **sentence** _____ a verb. (has, have)

2. **You** _____ basketball on television. (watches, watch)

3. Some **players** often _____ the ball. (dunks, dunk)

4. **Roger** _____ at the corner grocery store. (shops, shop)

5. Good **writers** _____ their paragraphs. (proofreads, proofread)

6. Usually **we** _____ salad with our dinner. (eats, eat)

7. **Roberta** _____ blood once a year. (gives, give)

8. **All** of the farmer's crops _____ to be watered. (needs, need)

9. Only **one** of my cousins _____ to that school. (goes, go)

10. **I** _____ a comedy to a drama. (prefers, prefer)

The most commonly confused verb is *be.*

Present Tense		**Past Tense**	
Singular	*Plural*	*Singular*	*Plural*
I am	we are	I was	we were
you are	you are	you were	you were
he, she, it is	they are	he, she, it was	they were

B Fill in each blank with the correct present tense form of *be.*

Donna _____ late. "Where _____ she?" her mother wonders. "Her brother

and sister _____ home."

Sharryl complains, "We _____ ready for dinner. The potatoes _____ cold.

The meat _____ cold, too. The bean casserole _____ ruined."

Donna walks through the door, and Mother says, "Donna, you _____ late again!"

Using Pronouns Correctly

A pronoun replaces a noun in a sentence.

An **antecedent** is the noun or noun and other pronoun that the pronoun stands for.

Rule 1: A pronoun must agree with its antecedent in number.

    Example: Harry drank a *soda* for lunch.

                    Harry drank *it* for lunch.

Soda is singular; therefore, the pronoun must be singular.

A Underline the pronoun in each sentence. Then write its antecedent on the line.

_____   **1.** Kenji went to the park with his friend Paco.

_____   **2.** Harry and Benita were late for their math class.

_____   **3.** Cathy has the flu, so she is staying home today.

_____   **4.** The assignment was difficult, but the students completed it.

_____   **5.** Josh and I went to the movies, and we saw two films.

Rule 2: A pronoun must agree with its antecedent in gender. The three genders are *feminine* (female), *masculine* (male), and *neuter* (neither female or male). If the noun used for a person does not indicate gender and does not refer to a specific person, you may wish to use both the masculine and feminine pronoun connected by the word *or*.

B Identify the gender of each pronoun in bold print. Write *Neuter, Masculine,* and/or *Feminine,* or on each line.

_____   **1.** The dog seems to have lost **its** bone.

_____   **2.** "Where is **she?**" wondered Heidi.

_____   **3.** Mario is doing **his** homework.

_____   **4.** Christine won **her** match in three sets.

_____   **5.** An unidentified witness told what **he or she** saw.

_____   **6.** Sharelle handed in **her** homework early.

_____   **7.** Abdul gave **his** old racket away.

_____   **8.** Has the cat eaten all of **its** food?

_____   **9.** The child left **his or her** jacket in school.

_____   **10.** Please place the book on **its** shelf.

The Case of the Pronoun

Rule 3: Different pronouns are used in place of subject, object, and possessive nouns. The form of the pronoun used depends on where it is used. Subject pronouns are used as subjects, object pronouns are used as objects, and possessive pronouns are used as possessives.

	Subject	Object	Possessive
	I	me	my, mine
	you	you	your, yours
Singular	he	him	his
	she	her	her, hers
	it	it	its
	we	us	our, ours
Plural	you	you	your, yours
	they	them	their, theirs

Example   I gave my mother a card on **her** birthday.

(*Mother* is the antecedent of *her*. The pronoun *her* shows possession and is a replacement for the possessive noun *mother's*.)

A Complete each sentence with the correct pronoun.

1. After school, Anton went to _____ job at the restaurant. (he, him, his)

2. Carol and _____ friend Emma will be here soon. (she, her, hers)

3. I got a perfect score on _____ test. (I, me, my, mine)

4. Hector and Luis work at the gas station, but _____ have different hours. (they, them, their, theirs)

5. Tinise and I won the science prize, and Mr. Stoley congratulated _____ . (we, us, our, ours)

B Check that the pronouns in the paragraph below are in the proper form. Correct any errors that you find.

   Mickey and me love to go swimming. The lifeguards at the pool sit in his

chair. They watch all of we swimmers carefully. One of the guards named

Donna is a good friend. He gave me swimming lessons many years ago. Now

she is encouraging Mickey and I to become lifeguards. Maybe, we will.

Plurals and Possessives

One of the most confusing things about the English language is recognizing the difference between a plural and a possessive. They sound alike but have different meanings.

Plural noun:	The **dancers** awed the audience.
Possessive noun:	The **dancer's** routine awed the audience.

To complicate matters, a possessive noun can also be plural.

Possessive plural:	The **dancers'** routine awed the audience.

Rules: Make a singular noun possessive by adding apostrophe -s ('s). Don't forget the apostrophe! (The **dog's** bark was very shrill.)

Make a plural noun that ends in s possessive by adding only an apostrophe ('). (The **horses'** coats were all groomed.)

Make a plural noun that does not end in s possessive by adding apostrophe -s ('s). (The **children's** room is a mess!)

A Make each of the nouns below possessive. Write the new word on the line.

1. Clarissa _____
2. trees _____
3. church _____
4. books _____
5. Arnold _____

6. mice _____
7. teeth _____
8. friend _____
9. Wilson _____
10. boss _____

B Decide whether the noun in bold print is singular, plural, singular possessive, or plural possessive. Write your answer on the line. The first item is done for you as an example.

singular possessive

_____ 1. The **dog's** treat is in the box.

_____ 2. My **feet** were sore after the long hike.

_____ 3. The **women's** team won all its games.

_____ 4. I stayed at my **friend's** house overnight.

_____ 5. This **racket** has loose strings.

_____ 6. The **Martinezes'** party was terrific.

_____ 7. We saw three **moose** in the field.

_____ 8. The **kitten's** mittens were lost.

Using Verbs Correctly: Verb Tense

Every sentence has a verb. Effective writers use verbs correctly. They are especially careful about tense. The word **tense** means "time." Verbs allow us to express when something happened in sentences.

You can change the tense of a verb in two ways:
- Add a suffix. (We usually add *-ed* to express past tense.)
- Use a helping verb. (We use *will* to express future tense.)

Verbs can express many different tenses. Here are the simple tenses.

Present	Tony **goes** to Barton Senior High School.
Past	Claudia **graduated** from the school last year.
Future	Next year Jackie **will enroll** in the school.

Use the **perfect tense** when you write about events that have already been completed.

Present Perfect	Paul **has** already **completed** college.
Past Perfect	Jason **had finished** high school three years before.
Future Perfect	Marietta **will have graduated** one year ago this June.

Underline the verb or verb phrase in each sentence. Write the verb tense on the line.

_____ 1. Find the verb in this sentence.

_____ 2. Erica will leave at noon.

_____ 3. Cassie read several books last summer.

_____ 4. Henri will probably go to Montana in March.

_____ 5. Yesterday Juan walked to the lake.

_____ 6. Has Hans called yet?

_____ 7. Mai had finished her work by noon.

_____ 8. Wilson will have probably gone by now.

_____ 9. Will you pass the butter, Nora?

_____ 10. Silvia worked very hard on the project.

_____ 11. At last, Nathan has arrived at the party.

_____ 12. Tomorrow, Aponi will be sixteen years old.

Progressive Tenses

When we write about ongoing events, we use the progressive tense. To form this tense, we use helping verbs and the suffix -ing.

Present Progressive	At this moment Dad **is walking** out the door.
Past Progressive	Ralph **was getting** ready for school.
Future Progressive	Next month Andrea **will be going** to camp.

You can also form *progressive perfect* tenses.

Present Perfect Progressive	Mitch **has been riding** all morning.
Past Perfect Progressive	April **had been swimming** for an hour when I saw her.
Future Perfect Progressive	Jan **will have been sleeping** for two hours by the time I arrive.

A Underline the verb or verb phrase in each sentence. Write the verb tense on the line.

_____ 1. Art is going to the beach this weekend.

_____ 2. The radio was blaring from the house across the street.

_____ 3. Angelique is teaching her little brother to swim.

_____ 4. Have you ever been surfing?

_____ 5. By noon, Georgia had been sewing for hours.

_____ 6. Will you be leaving soon?

_____ 7. Matt will have been living there for six weeks next Friday.

_____ 8. The carpenters are building a new house.

_____ 9. Joy is writing her autobiography.

_____ 10. Had you ever been fishing before this trip?

B Find the verb in each sentence below. Identify it as present tense, past tense, future tense, perfect tense, or progressive tense.

_____ 1. George Washington was President of the United States.

_____ 2. Have you ever studied about him?

_____ 3. My class will study about him next week.

_____ 4. Other classes have been reading about him, too.

_____ 5. George Washington's lovely home is in Mt. Vernon.

_____ 6. We are visiting it next summer.

Conditional Tenses

There are also **conditional** tenses. We use helping verbs to form the conditional tenses.

Conditional   Jane **may be** here soon.
                    Ahmed **should mow** the yard.

Conditional Perfect   **Could** Hugo **have** already **gone**?
                    Kuaku **may have** finally **completed** that novel.

A Underline the verb or verb phrase in each sentence. Write the verb tense on the line.

1. Would you turn on the radio, Tom?
2. Jason must finish his math now.
3. Carmen and Iris might go to the movies later.
4. The apartment should be ready soon.
5. Paulina's typewriter must be new.
6. Could you pass these papers out?
7. I can name that tune in three notes.
8. May I have the vegetables please?
9. Sean must have finished his chores.
10. Could Jeanne have already left?

Another verb tense is the **emphatic** tense. This tense is formed with the verb *do*.
We also use *do* to ask questions.

      Present—**Do** you **like** to watch sports on television?

      Past—Dave **did** not **finish** his work.

B Underline the verb phrase in each sentence. Write *Past* or *Present* on the line.

1. Did you lose your book?
2. Christopher did not want any lemonade.
3. The students do use the computer every day.
4. Did your team compete in the tournament?
5. Does Tubbs wash or dry the dishes?
6. Usually the stores do remain open on weekends.

Logical Verb Tense

When you write a sentence, the verb tense must be logical. *Logical* means "making sense."

Wrong:	Yesterday we will move into new offices.
Right:	Tomorrow we will move into new offices.
Right:	Yesterday we moved into new offices.

The adverb *yesterday* refers to the past; therefore, the verb must be past tense. The adverb *tomorrow* refers to the future; therefore, the verb must be the future tense.

A Underline the verbs in each sentence. Decide if the tense of each verb is logical. Correct any mistakes you find.

Yesterday, Tara and Keir will miss the awards show on television. Tara wanted to know who win. Tara looked for the newspaper. It has a list of all the winners.

"Have you seen today's newspaper?" Tara asked Keir.

"It is here a minute ago," said Keir.

"You have the paper earlier," said Tara. "Where do you put it?"

B Underline the verb or verb phrase in each sentence. Write the verb tense on the line.

_____ 1. Could you call me after work?

_____ 2. Where do you do your laundry?

_____ 3. Have you ever eaten at that restaurant?

_____ 4. Roberto had read fifty-seven books at last count.

_____ 5. The dogs were barking at the postal carrier.

_____ 6. Who is knocking at the door?

_____ 7. Opal finally wrote a letter to Bonnie.

_____ 8. Donna was playing golf this afternoon.

_____ 9. Do you buy popcorn at the movies?

_____ 10. That movie had a surprise ending.

Comparisons

Adverbs and adjectives have three forms: **Positive**, **Comparative**, and **Superlative**.

Rule 1: For many shorter adjectives and adverbs, *-er* is added to form the comparative and *-est* is added to form the superlative. If the word ends in *e,* drop the *e* before adding the suffix. If the word ends in consonant *y,* change the *y* to *i* before adding the suffix. It the word is a one syllable word that ends with a single consonant, double the consonant before adding the suffix.

small	smaller	smallest	happy	happier	happiest
nice	nicer	nicest	hot	hotter	hottest

Rule 2: Use the *comparative* to compare two things. Use the *superlative* to compare three or more things.

Examples: Aaron is **taller** than Mike. Of the three brothers, Corey is the **tallest**.

Rule 3: With many longer adjectives and adverbs that end in *-ly,* usually use *more* to form the comparative and *most* to form the superlative.

exciting	more exciting	most exciting
slowly	more slowly	most slowly

Rule 4: A few adjectives and adverbs are irregular. Check your dictionary for the comparative and superlative forms.

good	better	best	bad	worse	worst

A Write the comparative and superlative forms of these adjectives and adverbs.

	Comparative	Superlative
1. accurate	_____	_____
2. cozy	_____	_____
3. red	_____	_____
4. courteous	_____	_____
5. large	_____	_____
6. quickly	_____	_____

B Complete each sentence with the correct adjective or adverb.

1. Raul is one of the _____ students in the class. (better, best)

2. Of the two girls, Francine is the _____ swimmer. (faster, fastest)

3. Who is the _____ swimmer on the team? (faster, fastest)

4. Is Kareem _____ than Saliha? (younger, youngest)

5. Which of the rings is the _____ expensive? (more, most)

Starting a Sentence

Adverbs and prepositional phrases are great for adding variety to sentences. They can be moved around in the sentence without changing its meaning.

Usually Jake likes apples. Jake **usually** likes apples.

The same thing can be done with prepositional phrases used as adverbs. A comma is needed after a prepositional phrase that begins a sentence or clause.

We go to the beach **in the summer**.

In the summer, we go to the beach.

The adverb or prepositional phrase in each sentence below is in bold. Move it to a different position in the sentence. Rewrite the sentence in the space below.

1. Meet me at the recreation center **after school.**

   _____

2. The children **eagerly** climbed aboard the roller coaster.

   _____

3. Our dog greeted us **enthusiastically.**

   _____

4. **By ten o'clock,** the morning rush hour is usually over.

   _____

5. **For her part in that movie,** Merryl Streep won an academy award.

   _____

6. I am going to Florida **on my next vacation.**

   _____

7. Did I fill out this form **correctly?**

   _____

8. **Carefully,** Miguel drove around the barriers on the obstacle course.

   _____

9. **During the night,** two inches of rain fell.

   _____

10. **With our help,** Carrie can **quickly** finish painting the room.

   _____

Review: Proofread, Revise, Recopy

 Follow the directions.

- Proofread the following paragraph carefully.
- Correct any mistakes you find.
- Move some adverbs and prepositional phrases to the beginning of the sentences for variety.
- Then recopy the paragraph with your changes.
- Check closely for the following errors:

  Subject-verb agreement

  Correct use of pronouns

  Plurals and possessives, including apostrophes

  Verb tense errors, especially verb endings

  Comparison forms of adverbs and adjectives

Booker T. Washington

Booker T. Washington is born a slave in 1856 in Hale's Ford, Virginia. After slavery were abolished, his mother moved the family to West Virginia. Because the family was poor, Washington have to start working when he is only nine years old. Washington worked at a salt furnace during the day and studied at night. He was finally able to enroll at Hampton Institute in Virginia in 1872. There him study to be a teacher. He worked as a janitor to pay for his room and board. He also attended Wayland Seminary in Washington, D.C. Booker T. Washington headed Tuskegee Institute, a teacher's college. The school became highly respected under his' leadership. He also was an influential leader of African Americans. He even advised several Presidents'. If you wants to read more about this remarkable man, read Washingtons autobiography, *Up From Slavery*. Booker T. Washington died in 1915.

Using a Dictionary

A dictionary contains so much information.

- Spelling and meaning of words
- Plural and other forms of a word
- Parts of speech
- Syllables and pronunciation
- Synonyms and antonyms
- History of words (**etymology**)

- Abbreviations
- Names of important people
- Facts about famous places
- Facts about mythology
- Names of some fictional characters
- And more!

Words in a dictionary are in alphabetical order. A word is found by using the guide words at the top of the page. The first guide word is the first entry on the page. The second guide word is the last entry on the page.

Study the guide words and page numbers below. For each word listed below, write the page where it can be found.

Page	Guide Words	Page	Guide Words
430	packager and Pakistani	433	pantomime and paradise
431	pal and pamper	434	paradox and parchment
432	pamphlet and panther		

_____ 1. paraphrase   _____ 9. pancake   _____ 17. Paine, Thomas

_____ 2. parameter   _____ 10. pantry   _____ 18. pajamas

_____ 3. parakeet   _____ 11. pain   _____ 19. Palm Springs

_____ 4. Panama   _____ 12. paper clip   _____ 20. paddock

_____ 5. paddle   _____ 13. Paiute   _____ 21. Paget, Sir James

_____ 6. panel   _____ 14. paprika   _____ 22. pantry

_____ 7. paltry   _____ 15. panic   _____ 23. parboil

_____ 8. papaya   _____ 16. palace   _____ 24. paramecium

Dictionary Entries

Let's examine the parts of a dictionary entry closely.

> **pe•tit four** (pet′ ē fôr′) *n., pl.* **pe•tits fours** (pet′ ē fôrz′);
>
> **pe•tit fours** (pet′ ē fôrz′) [*Fr.,* lit., small oven] a small frosted cake

- The new word begins the entry.
- The pronunciation is in parentheses.
- The plural form is given only if it is irregular.
- The etymology (history of the word) is given.
- The meaning of the word is provided.

A Use the information above to answer these questions.

1. Would people eat a petit four? _____

2. What does the word *petit four* mean in French? _____

3. What are the plural forms of the word? _____

4. What part of speech is the word? _____

5. What do you think *petit* means? _____

B Use the information in the entries below to answer the questions.

> **pet•ty cash** *n.* a cash fund from which small incidental expenses
>   are paid
>
> **Pfc, Pfc., PFC** *Private First Class*
>
> **Phar•aoh** (fer′ō) *n.* the title of the rulers of ancient Egypt
>
> **phar•ma•cy** (fär′m ə sē) *n., pl.* **-cies 1.** the art or profession of
>   preparing and dispensing drugs and medicines **2.** a drug store
>
> **Phil•ip•pines** (fil′ ə pēnz′) country occupying a group of *c.* 7,100
>   islands (**Philippine Islands**) in the SW Pacific off the SE coast of
>   Asia; 114,830 sq. mi.; pop. 38,613,000; cap. Manila

1. What did the ancient Egyptians call their rulers? _____

2. Approximately how many islands make up the Philippines? _____

3. Another word for *pharmacy* is _____.

4. Get the money for stamps out of _____.

5. What does *PFC* stand for? _____

6. How many syllables does *pharmacy* have? _____

The Thesaurus

A **thesaurus** is a book of synonyms and antonyms. Many thesauruses list the entries in alphabetical order just as dictionaries do. Some, however, arrange the entries by subject. A thesaurus with entries arranged by subject has an index. You use the index to find the word you are interested in. The number beside the word is the entry number. You locate the word by its entry number.

> *Sample entry:*
> **prude** 903
> **prudent** cautious 895
> **prudish** fastidious 896
>
> **prune** cut off 42
> **pry**
>   v. be inquisitive 528
>   investigate 485

A Write the page number of the following entries. Use the sample index above.

1. *prudent* meaning "cautious" _____

2. *prune* meaning "to cut off" _____

3. *prudish* meaning "fastidious" _____

4. *prudent* meaning "cautious" _____

5. *prude* _____

➤ A thesaurus also may list foreign words and phrases.

➤ A thesaurus may include a list of abbreviations.

B Complete each sentence with the correct abbreviation or foreign phrase.

Foreign Words and Phrases	Abbreviations
au revoir—until we meet again	A.D. Anno Domini (Latin; in the year of our Lord)
bon voyage—a good journey to you	I.O.U.—I owe you
cul-de-sac—a blind alley	J.P.—Justice of the Peace

1. George was born in _____ 1912.

2. The children waved good-bye and said, "_____."

3. When Timmy borrowed money, he wrote out an _____.

4. As the ship sailed, our friends on the dock shouted "_____."

5. We live at the end of the _____.

6. Wendy and Aaron got married by a _____.

Sample Entry

Study the information about a thesaurus.

- Within an entry, terms are organized by part of speech.

- Semicolons separate groups of words that are closest in meaning.

- The boldface words are key words that indicate the general meaning of the synonyms following.

- The entries include cross-references to related words.

- Major entries include cross-references to antonyms.

Sample Entry

NEARNESS.—I. *Nouns.* **nearness,** closeness, proximity, short distance, short way, little ways; close quarters.
nearby region, vicinity, neighborhood, environs.
II. *Verbs.* **Be near,** border on, neighbor; adjoin, lie next to, border, abut.
near, near or close, approach, approximate, border on, verge on.
III. *Adjectives.* **near,** close, neighboring, approximate, convenient, handy, at hand, easily reached.
next, abutting, adjacent side by side.
intimate, close, dear, familiar.
IV. *Adverbs, phrases.* **near,** nigh, close, at close quarters; nearby, next door to, in sight of.
nearly, approximately, almost.
See also APPROACH, EASE, ENVIRONMENT, RELATIONSHIP, SIMILARITY, TOUCH.
Antonyms—See DISTANCE.

A Use the sample entry to write a synonym for "nearness" for each part of speech.

1. noun _____   **3.** adjective _____

2. verb _____   **4.** adverb _____

B Fill in each blank with an appropriate word from the sample entry.

1. The baseball park is in this _____. (noun)

2. Being at such _____ makes me claustrophobic. (noun)

3. The lot _____ a large forest preserve. (verb)

4. The store's _____ location makes it easy for me to stop and pick up a few items. (adjective)

5. The bank is _____ the police station. (adverb)

Review: Proofread, Revise, Recopy

 Follow the directions.

- Proofread the following paragraph carefully. Use a dictionary and a thesaurus to help you find the best words to express the ideas.

- Then recopy the paragraph with your changes.

- Check closely for the following error: Exact meaning of words.

- **Hint:** Look up the words below in a thesaurus. Find a synonym that has a more precise or interesting meaning.

childhood	really	told	shivers
think	liked	gather	laugh
stories	scary	character	special

Stories by Aunt Jeanne

Whenever I think about my childhood summers, I think about my aunt and her stories. Aunt Jeanne came home every summer to visit the family. She was the best storyteller I knew. My brother, sister, and I really liked the scary stories she told. She would gather us on a bed and darken the room. Then she made up stories about a character named Old Mr. Norstrom. As she told the stories, I could feel the hair raise on the back of my neck, and my brother, sister, and I would shiver and scream. Now I laugh when Aunt Jeanne tells the same special stories to my children.

_____

_____

_____

_____

_____

_____

Writing Paragraphs

A **paragraph** is a group of related sentences about one main idea. Paragraphs often have two main parts:

- a topic sentence
- related sentences

Sometimes, a paragraph also has a conclusion or summary.

The hardest part of writing is always getting started, even for professional writers. When you get stuck, ask yourself these questions:

Why am I writing this paragraph? What do I want to say?

Just "talk to yourself." You can't write without information to write about. You need to trust your own ideas. Your ideas come from many places:

from your personal experiences

from reading what others have written

from information other people have given you

from watching videos, movies, and television programs

from thinking about all those things and what they mean

Make a list of topics that you might like to write about someday. Use your imagination! Save the list for later.

Examples: My Most Unforgettable Person, My Geometry Teacher!
Training My Labrador Retriever How to Speak

Your List

_____

_____

_____

_____

_____

 For You to Do: If you want to be a writer, you must write! Write every day for a few minutes. Keep a journal. Starting tonight, write a few sentences about your day. Don't worry about proofreading, revising, and recopying. Just write!

Topic Sentences

A **topic sentence** gives the main idea of a paragraph.

- Writers express the main idea of a paragraph in a topic sentence.
- Writers may express their point of view in the topic sentence.
- A topic sentence often is a general statement.
- Often the topic sentence is the first sentence in a paragraph.

 Read the following paragraph. Then answer the questions.

      A Labrador retriever is not an easy dog to train. I know because I have a chocolate Lab puppy whose name is Bully. First, I taught Bully to sit. Then for several weeks, I tried to teach Bully to speak. Bully sat and watched with doleful eyes while I said, "Speak" over and over until I was hoarse. Bully just looked at me and never once barked. Our poodle, who had already been trained, barked and barked while Bully stayed silent. One day Bully suddenly figured it out and barked. I praised him with great enthusiasm. There is only one problem. Now, whenever I say, "Sit" or "Speak," Bully sits down and barks. As I said, training a Lab is a challenge.

1. Which sentence in the paragraph is the topic sentence?

   _____

2. Which statement best sums up the writer's point of view. Circle your answer.

   a. Labrador retrievers are fast learners.

   b. Poodles are smarter than Labrador retrievers.

   c. Labrador retrievers are difficult to train.

   d. The writer was not a very good dog trainer.

3. How does the writer back up his or her point of view?

   _____

4. What is this paragraph about?

   _____

5. Write a title for this paragraph that sums up the main idea.

   _____

6. Write another topic sentence for this paragraph.

   _____

7. Did you enjoy reading this paragraph? Explain why or why not.

   _____

   _____

Supporting the Main Idea

Paragraphs always express a main idea. A writer may write a topic sentence that expresses the main idea of a paragraph. A writer's job is to develop the main idea in the paragraph. Sentences that tell more details about the main idea make up the body of the paragraph. The body of the paragraph should always include sentences that relate to the main idea.

A well-developed paragraph may have between three and seven sentences. If a paragraph becomes very long, it may become difficult to read. A writer can avoid overlong paragraphs by dividing ideas into subtopics.

A Develop a body of a paragraph that supports the topic sentence below. Use the information in the box. Write at least three sentences.

Hint: Watch out for run-on sentences and sentence fragments!

> **Education of a Dentist**
> high school   internship
> college with a science   residency to study
> major   a specialty
> dental school

A dentist needs a lot of education. _____

_____

_____

_____

_____

_____

_____

B All of the sentences in the paragraph should be about the main idea. Find the sentence that doesn't fit, and cross it out.

Tennis has been Kelly's favorite sport since she was eleven. She likes to play tennis with her friends on weekends. Kelly is also on her high school tennis team, and she has played in many tournaments. Her racket broke last week, and she got a new one. Kelly will probably continue playing this game for many years.

Adding Details and Examples

Writers support their ideas with details and examples. Suppose you start with this topic sentence:

> *Whenever I see a wrestling match, I think of my high school geometry teacher.*

That's a good start. You have introduced the topic. Now you need to explain why you connect wrestling with this teacher.

> *Mr. McNelis was not only an excellent math teacher, but also the wrestling coach. He loved the sport and talked a lot about it. The year I took geometry, his team won the state championship. He gave all students extra credit in geometry if they attended the matches! I could always use the extra credit, so I never missed an event.*

OK, now we see the connection between geometry and wrestling. Now we need one more sentence—one that sums up the main idea again.

> *To this day when a wrestling match is on television, the Pythagorean theorem pops into my head, and I remember Mr. McNelis!*

■ Write your own paragraph. Choose one of the topics below or make up one of your own. Start with a topic sentence. Explain the topic with examples or details. Write a sentence at the end that "sums up" the topic.

Suggested Topics

A Pet to Remember   Sports Hero   My Best Friend   The Best Day Yet

_____

_____

_____

_____

_____

_____

_____

Conclusions and Summaries

The last sentence in your paragraph may be a **conclusion** or a **summary**.

A *conclusion* is "the end." It may be a judgment or opinion that your formed after your examined some facts. The conclusion of your paragraph should be logical. A conclusion may follow the term "therefore" or "in conclusion."

A *summary* is a brief report covering the main points. The last sentence of a paragraph could simply restate the main idea that you expressed in the topic sentence.

That is why I think of Mr. McNelis every time I see a wrestling match!

Write a summary statement for each of the following paragraphs.

1. Since I started using a computer, writing has become easier. With the computer, I can add and delete words. I can correct mistakes. I can even move sentences around. I can use the spell-check to find and correct misspellings. With a computer, I don't need erasers. I don't have to recopy what I have written.

_____

_____

_____

_____

_____

2. For as long as I can remember, I have loved to read. When Mom used to read to me at night, I would ask if I could read to her. Then I would make up a story that went with the pictures in the book. After I finally learned to read, I would read everything I could get my hands on. Books, cereal boxes, and road signs were among my reading materials. I still enjoy reading today. In fact, I am a first grade reading teacher, and I enjoy teaching reading, too.

_____

_____

_____

_____

_____

UNIT 6

Effective writers stay with the point they are trying to make. Sometimes, however, it is easy to get off the subject. Always remember that writers start with a **draft**. Then, they proofread, revise, and recopy. Nobody is expected to write a perfect paragraph on the first try.

An **extraneous** statement is one that doesn't relate to the rest of the paragraph. It doesn't support the main idea. It doesn't fit in.

But that was my favorite sentence.

Sorry, but it was extraneous!

Read each paragraph below. Cross out any extraneous sentence or sentences.

1. Most high school students take a course in geometry. It is a branch of mathematics dealing with the properties, measurements, and relationships of points, lines, planes, and solids. Students study propositions and theorems. A *proposition* is simply a problem to be solved. A *theorem* is a mathematical law or a basic principle. A proposition can be proved from accepted premises, and in geometry class, students figure out how to prove propositions in logical steps. My geometry teacher's name was Ms. Nardini. One of the main benefits of studying geometry is learning to think logically.

2. New Mexico is called the "Land of Enchantment." To *enchant* means "to cast a spell over someone because of great charm or delight." There are many wonderful places to visit in this state. The population is more than a million people. People love to visit its eighteen million acres of forest land. Ponderosa pine and Douglas fir enhance the countryside. New Mexico boasts the largest natural cave "room" in the world. Another delightful feature of the state is its dry comfortable climate. Perhaps that is why tourism is one of New Mexico's most important industries.

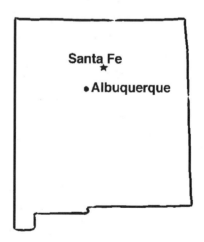

Review: Proofread, Revise, Recopy

■ Follow the directions.

- Write a paragraph.
- *Proofread* your paragraph carefully.
- Revise you paragraph.
- Then *recopy* the paragraph with your changes.
- Check closely for the following errors:
  Parts of a paragraph   Sentence structure

Hint: Write an interesting title for your paragraph.

Suggested Topics

My Dream House	The Ideal Vacation	My Goals
Computer Fun	The Best Movie Ever	Stories in the News

First Draft

_____

_____

_____

_____

_____

_____

_____

_____

Final Copy

_____

_____

_____

_____

_____

_____

_____

_____

Rewriting

Students often write reports. They gather information for their reports from books, magazines, newspapers, and encyclopedias. Here are one student's sample notes.

Jimmie Foxx (1907–1967); Red Sox, Athletics slugger; Hall of Fame; MVP 3 times—1932 and 1933, Philadelphia Athletics and 1938, Boston; triple crown, 1933, Philadelphia Athletics. A triple crown winner leads the league in runs batted in, batting average, and home runs in a single season. Foxx led the American League in home runs 4 times: in 1932, 58 homers, only 3 behind Roger Maris's all-time record of 61. In 1933, he hit 48; in 1935, he hit 36; and in 1939, he hit 35. Foxx holds third place in home runs hit in a single year behind Roger Maris and Babe Ruth. He is ninth for lifetime home runs with 534. He won the batting title twice; in 1933, he batted .356; in 1938, he batted .349.

This is the paragraph the student wrote.

Jimmie Foxx, Hall of Famer

Baseball fans in the 1930s had the privilege of seeing one of the all-time great sluggers, Jimmie Foxx. While he was with the Philadelphia Athletics, he was voted the American League's most valuable player in both 1932 and 1933. When he played for the Boston Red Sox in 1936, he won this award again. Foxx is best known as a home run hitter, leading the league with most homers in a single year four times. His greatest achievement came in 1933 when he won the triple crown—most runs batted in, most home runs, and highest batting average. Seeing Jimmie Foxx playing baseball must have been a truly outstanding experience.

■ Use the sample notes to write your own paragraph. Do your work on a separate sheet of paper.

A dictionary definition tells you what a word means. You can demonstrate that you understand the meaning by putting the definition in your own words. This is a good practice for writing effective paragraphs.

> **spear grass** any of several perennial grasses (genus *Stipa*) having hard, sharp-pointed, bearded fruit

Often one definition leads you to another. For example, what does *perennial* mean?

> **perennial** *adj.* **1.** lasting or active throughout the whole year **2.** lasting or continuing for a long time [a *perennial* youth] **3.** returning or becoming active again and again; perpetual **4.** having a life cycle of more than two years; said especially of plants that produce flowers and seed from the same root structure year after year

What is *spear grass*?

> *Spear grass* is a type of grass that lives all year long. Its fruit is hard with sharp points and appears to be bearded.

Look up the following words in a dictionary. Rewrite the definitions in your own words.

pennyroyal   pen pal   pension   pentagon   Pentagon

1. What is a *pennyroyal?*

_____

_____

2. What is a *pen pal?*

_____

_____

3. What is a *pension?*

_____

_____

4. What is a *pentagon?*

_____

_____

5. What is a *Pentagon?*

_____

_____

Spice It Up!

Writers can make facts interesting to read. The key is choosing words carefully. Compare these two sentences.

Flying fishes live in the ocean where they can be seen swimming about near boats.

Flying fishes are **oceanic species** often seen **skittering** near boats.

skitter   to skip or move along quickly and lightly

oceanic   living in the ocean

species   a distinct kind, sort, or type

Rewrite each sentence. Use more colorful vocabulary. You may add words or replace words. Use a dictionary or a thesaurus.

1. A dictionary is a useful book for writers.

_____

_____

2. Betina played basketball in the city park often.

_____

_____

3. A tuna is a member of the mackerel family that swims in schools and migrates on irregular paths and schedules.

_____

_____

4. A compact disc (CD) player produces high-quality sound using a digital recording method.

_____

_____

5. *Jurassic Park* was a hit movie in 1993.

_____

_____

6. Mr. McNelis is a geometry teacher with an interest in wrestling.

_____

_____

Review: Paraphrasing

 Follow the directions.

- Rewrite the story below. Put it in your own words.
- Use a dictionary and a thesaurus to improve the sentences.

The Night I Almost Scored a Basket

To tell the truth, I'm not much of an athlete. Last winter I joined a basketball team, anyway. It was just for fun. The first thing I noticed was that I couldn't run up and down the court without being out of breath. I started jogging every day, and soon I could keep up with the others. I also noticed that I couldn't get the basketball into the hoop. I practiced for at least an hour every night until I could at least make some baskets.

My one great fear was that I would be fouled in the game and have to make a free throw. Sure enough, during the first game, a player on the other team fouled me. I prepared to take my free throw. My heart was pounding so loudly that I couldn't hear the fans screaming. I lined up my shot and threw the ball with all my strength, just like I had practiced. The ball hit the backboard lightly and then rolled slowly around the rim. For a few seconds, the suspense mounted. Then, alas, the ball fell to the floor without going through the hoop. To my surprise, the fans gave me a loud ovation. Everyone was surprised that I had come so close to making the basket. I was very pleased but took great care not to let anyone foul me again.

_____

_____

_____

_____

_____

_____

_____

_____

U N I T 1

A In each sentence, circle the word in parentheses that is correct.

1. Last week, Darren (go, went, gone) to the basketball camp at the recreation center.

2. Kathryn (sing, sings, sung) the part of Annie in the musical play.

3. Shanell finished (she, her, hers) homework during study hall.

4. Did you go with (they, them, their) on the roller coaster?

5. (Beth, Beths, Beth's) first class is at eight o'clock.

6. The bus (has been, should have been, will be) here fifteen minutes ago.

7. I have never before seen a (spectacularer, more spectacular, most spectacular) sunset.

8. The queen asked, "Who is the (fair, fairer, fairest) of all?"

9. Ms. Chambers and (I, me, my) work in the same office building.

10. Either Karyn or Sam (is, are, was) next in line for a promotion.

B Write a paragraph about one of your own experiences or something that interests you. Choose a topic and write a topic sentence. Make sure all the sentences in the body of your paragraph are related to the topic. Close your paragraph with a summary or concluding statement. Make sure you use verb tense and pronouns correctly. Use a dictionary and a thesaurus to make sure you are using the most appropriate and descriptive words in your paragraph.

_____

_____

_____

_____

_____

_____

_____

_____

_____

_____

_____

The Descriptive Approach

Descriptive writing is like using words to paint a picture. An artist uses colors and a paint brush. A writer uses colorful words and a pen. Effective writers create pictures with words by adding details. To write about detail, you must first be **observant**. *Observant* means "to look or feel closely."

A Make a list of descriptive words and phrases for each word in bold print. Examples have been given for you.

1. **Colors:** metallic, lemon yellow, _____

_____

2. **Textures:** velvety, slimy, _____

_____

3. **Temperatures:** icy, steamy, _____

_____

4. **Sounds:** scratchy, thunderous,_____

_____

5. **Sights:** tattered, transparent, _____

_____

6. **Tastes:** salty, delicious, _____

_____

B Read the following descriptive phrases. You should get a mental picture of the object being described. Then, look at any object around you and use words and phrases to describe it. Do not use sentences or paragraphs.

   Lamp: pale white shade with brown flecks running vertically; sculptured, brown wooden base; dark pine color; glass bulb glowing in the dark

Object: _____

_____

_____

_____

Using Adjectives and Adverbs

Adjectives are words that modify nouns and pronouns. They help us describe in more detail the subjects we write about. Adjectives help us answer the questions *Which one? How many? What kind?*

A Write a paragraph about an object that you see around you. Add as many adjectives as you can. Be sure that your paragraph still makes sense, of course!

Suggested Items for Topics

a window in the room	a vase with flowers	a desk or chair
the view outside the window	a pencil	a book

_____

_____

_____

_____

_____

_____

_____

_____

_____

B Guess the type of animal from the following description.

Behind my house is a small stand of trees where a tiny animal lives. It has a bushy tail and light and dark brown stripes down the middle of its back and head. It lives in burrows underground, and it fills its cheeks with food when it eats. Sometimes it visits my bird feeder, where it collects seeds and takes them back to its burrow. I love to see it scurrying past me as it scampers away!

The animal is a _____ .

C Write a description of an animal. Do your work on a separate sheet of paper. Go into detail but do not mention the animal's name. Read your description to a friend. See if your friend can guess the animal.

Similes and Metaphors

A **simile** is an indirect comparison. (Soren is as jumpy as a frog.) (The kite is like an eagle riding the air currents.) It uses the words *like* or *as*.

A **metaphor** is a direct comparison. (Antonio is a bear when he first wakes up.)

A Explain each of these sentences. Write your answer on each line.

Similes

1. Cal's hands are as rough as sandpaper. _____

_____

2. Suzanne is as tall as the Eiffel Tower. _____

_____

Metaphors

3. All the world's a stage. _____

_____

4. Cassie is a hot pan of boiling water. _____

_____

B Write five examples of similes and five examples of metaphors.

Similes

1. _____
2. _____
3. _____
4. _____
5. _____

Metaphors

6. _____
7. _____
8. _____
9. _____
10. _____

Personification

UNIT 8

When we attribute human qualities to objects, animals, or ideas, we are using **personification.** Sometimes personification helps us effectively create a picture with words.

> The moonbeam danced gleefully around my room.

> The mice played a game of hide and seek with the cat.

A Write your own examples of personification.

1. _____

2. _____

3. _____

4. _____

5. _____

B Read the following paragraph. Find examples of each figure of speech listed below. Write your answer on each line.

> Snowflakes are the earth's white, laced doilies. They are like a child's soap bubbles gently floating to the ground. They are the messengers of winter, but they give up their lives and die in the warm spring sun.

1. simile: _____

_____

_____

2. metaphor: _____

_____

_____

3. personification: _____

_____

_____

Review: Descriptive Writing

■ Follow the directions.

- Rewrite the story below in your own words.

- Add details. Use a dictionary and a thesaurus to improve the sentences.

- **Hints:**   Replace being verbs with action verbs.
                Use words that convey texture, color, scent, and feeling.

First Day at School

One of my most memorable experiences was my first day of school. I had been looking forward to kindergarten for a long time. My mother said I would learn to read. My dad told me about learning arithmetic. To tell you the truth, I was very frightened. In my mind, I would be coming home the first day with an armload of books and a long list of homework assignments. Well, do you know what we did? We played games, and the teacher read to us!

"How did it go?" my mother asked when I got home.

"It was easy!" I told her gleefully with a great sigh of relief.

_____

_____

_____

_____

_____

_____

_____

_____

_____

_____

_____

_____

The Expository Paragraph

An **expository paragraph** is a "detailed explanation" of something. It sets forth facts, information, and ideas. *Exposition* sets out to explain or define. Naturally, these paragraphs have a **topic sentence**, a **body**, and perhaps a **conclusion** or **summary**.

➤ The *topic sentence* identifies the main idea.

> *Expressing grief is essential for people to maintain good health.*

➤ The *body* explains the main idea.

> *The loss of someone we love can be a devastating experience. We must express our grief so that we can put the loss behind us. Everyone expresses grief differently. Some people find it easy to cry. Others try to deny the loss and hold back their tears. Eventually, however, they must deal with the truth.*

➤ The last sentence should sum up the ideas.

> So, *although people handle grief differently, everyone must eventually deal with losses.*

■ Write an expository paragraph about a topic of your choice.

_____

_____

_____

_____

_____

_____

_____

_____

_____

_____

_____

_____

_____

Happiness is...: Writing Definitions

One of the most common types of **expository writing** that we do is simply writing *definitions*. We can define a word by using only its **denotation** (the simple dictionary definition) or its **connotation** (the ideas and feelings associated with a word).

A Use a dictionary or your own experience to write a short definition of each of the following words.

1. *Nonsense* is _____

_____

2. *Perfume* is _____

_____

3. *Loyalty* is _____

_____

4. *Winning* is _____

_____

5. A *pet* is _____

_____

B Use a dictionary or your own experience to write an expository paragraph about one of the suggested topics below.

Suggested Topics

Bravery Is...   My Favorite Sandwich Is...

Friendship Is...   Youth Is...

_____

_____

_____

_____

_____

_____

_____

_____

The Book Report

A book report is usually *expository writing*. Expository writing provides information or gives an explanation. In a book report, your task is to tell about the book you have read. Your report should provide the following information:

Book Title:	Always include the complete title of the book, including the subtitle.
Author's Name:	Include the author's name.
Copyright Date and Publisher:	The date the book was published and the name of the publisher may be on the title page or on the copyright page. Include these in your report.
Characters:	Fictional books have characters. You may want to identify the names and a brief description of the main characters in your report. Nonfiction books may be about people also. If they are, be sure to name them and tell the role they played.
Plot:	What happened in this book? What's this book about? The plot is the story, the happenings in the book. Tell about the plot briefly. Put the events in *chronological order,* the way they happened.
Setting:	Where did the story take place? Describe the geography of the area, and whatever else the author told you about the location. Setting helps set up the tone, or *mood,* of the story.
Theme:	The theme of the book is the idea the author is trying to get across to the reader; it is the book's message. The theme should be a recurring idea that keeps coming up as you read the book. Not all books have a theme.

Use the information above to complete each sentence.

1. The person who wrote the book is the _____.

2. The main idea of the book is called the _____.

3. The _____ is the events of the book.

4. The order in which things happen is _____ order.

5. A book's _____ is the location in which the story took place.

6. Setting contributes to the _____ of a book.

7. The name of the book is its _____.

8. The date the book was published is its _____ date.

9. The copyright date may be found on the title page or the _____ page.

10. _____ writing is mainly a factual account of something.

Movie and TV Reviews

A movie or television review should be *expository writing*. Even though you give your opinions, you need to back them up with examples and details.

M.A.S.H.

M.A.S.H., the television program, was one of the most popular series ever produced. Its last episode had one of the largest audiences ever. The program was about a group of doctors and nurses who served in the armed forces during the Korean War. Alan Alda, who played Hawkeye Pierce, headed the outstanding cast, who portrayed doctors, nurses, and support personnel in a mobile hospital unit faced with the day-to-day burden of caring for the casualties of war. Although M.A.S.H. was about war and clearly illustrated the tragedy of war, the program was a comedy filled with the humor of everyday life. For example, B.J., Hawkeye's roommate turned to practical jokes to relieve the stress of overwork in less than desirable conditions. Among its most endearing qualities were the interactions among the main characters and the consistently true-to-life scripts. The success of M.A.S.H. has been acknowledged by its loyal fans who continue to watch reruns of the programs and by the awarding of a number of Emmy awards for the show and its cast members.

Revise and recopy the review of M.A.S.H. or write a review of a movie or television program of your choice.

_____

_____

_____

_____

_____

_____

_____

_____

_____

_____

_____

_____

_____

A well-known form of expository writing is the "How to ..." sentence, paragraph, or book. In this type of writing, you provide information about how to perform a task.

Topic Sentence:	Tell your reader what you are going to teach them.
Body:	Teach them, step by step.
Conclusion:	Tell them what they've got when they are finished.

How to Make an Omelet

Making an omelet is easy. Break two fresh eggs in a bowl. Add two tablespoons of water or milk. Season to taste. Beat with a wire whip. Prepare a frying pan by melting a small amount of margarine on medium heat. As soon as the margarine is melted, pour in the eggs and cover the pan if you wish. When the eggs are nearly set (firm), turn or flip them over. Then add any or all of the following ingredients or ingredients of your choice: grated cheese, crumbled bacon, chopped green pepper and onions, chopped tomatoes, and slices of fresh mushrooms. Fold the eggs in half over the added ingredients. Wait a few seconds, then place on a plate. Garnish with parsley and fresh fruit and serve with toast and orange juice. You will have an omelet that is not only tasty but beautiful to look at.

■ Choose one of the topics suggested below or use one of your own. Write step by step the directions to follow.

Suggested Topics

How to Tie a Tie   How to Make a Pot of Coffee

How to Pitch a Fastball   How to Serve an Ace in Tennis

How to Set the Table for an Elegant Dinner

_____

_____

_____

_____

_____

_____

_____

_____

_____

_____

_____

Review: Expository Writing

Follow the directions.

- Rewrite the following paragraph in your own words.

- Add details. Use a dictionary and a thesaurus.

- **Hints:**   Replace being verbs with action verbs.

    Be sure your sentence structure is correct; do not use run-on sentences.

    Check the topic and summary sentences carefully.

Zucchini

One of the easiest vegetables to grow in your garden is the versatile zucchini. Zucchini is a member of the summer squash family. It is green-skinned and shaped somewhat like a cucumber. Few garden plants grow as fast as this vegetable. It seems as though one day you have a yellow flower, and the next day, you have a tiny finger-long fruit. Within only a few days, a zucchini can get as big as a small watermelon! Zucchinis are delicious uncooked in salads or with dips, baked in bread, cooked with tomatoes, pickled like relishes, or stuffed like peppers. If you are looking for a vegetable that you can grow successfully and use in many ways, try zucchini.

Say What You Mean

The purpose of writing is to communicate your ideas to another person. Avoid **ambiguity**. *Ambiguous* writing could have more than one meaning, thus making writing vague, unclear, fuzzy, or obscure. Writing can be ambiguous for many reasons. Perhaps the antecedent of a pronoun is not clear. Maybe the verb tenses are incorrect. Run-on sentences or sentence fragments can make writing unclear. The lack of a topic sentence or extraneous information can also make writing ambiguous.

 Rewrite this paragraph to make it simpler and more direct. Take out all the words and phrases that don't mean anything.

Every colony of honey bees has worker bees. These are female bees that do all the work and never mate. Worker bees collect nectar from flowers and return it to the hive. There other workers add enzymes, and it becomes honey. The honey tastes good on toast and cereal. Drones live in the colony, too. The worker bees have to feed the drones because they do not have long enough tongues to drink the nectar from flowers. The only thing they do is mate with a queen bee. Drones never mate with the queen in their own hive. They always mate with queens from other hives. In the cooler months when food becomes scarce, the worker bees force the drones out of the hive, and they die. The queen bee has only one purpose. She lays eggs. These hatch into larva that the worker bees care for and then seal into cells of the hive. They grow into pupa and then become adults. The worker bees have other jobs too. They clean the hive, they put wax caps on the honey-filled cells of the hive, they guard the hive, and they scout for new places for new hives when the old one becomes crowded. I guess when we talk about being busy as a bee, we are talking about the worker bees.

_____

_____

_____

_____

_____

_____

_____

_____

_____

_____

_____

The Active Voice

One way to make your writing more effective is by using active voice verbs. In English, verbs have two voices—**active** and **passive**. The active voice tells what someone or something is doing or did. The doer of an action is the subject of a sentence with a verb in active voice. The passive voice emphasizes what is being done or was done. The receiver of the action or the action itself is the subject in passive voice.

    Active: John *hit* the baseball out of the park.

    Passive: The baseball *was hit* out of the park by John.

A Change the verbs in bold print from passive to active voice. Write each sentence on the line provided. Use the example above as a guide.

1. A tree on the golf course **was struck** by lightning.

_____

2. The horse **was ridden** in the show by an experienced rider.

_____

3. An excellent report **was given** by Christy Franklin.

_____

4. Jonine's short story **was published** in the *New Yorker* Magazine.

_____

5. Claudia **was pleased** by the critic's response to her new film.

_____

B Revise the following paragraph by changing the passive verbs to active voice. Recopy the improved paragraph.

    In that movie, the town's bank was robbed by a bandit, who was dressed all in black from his shoes to his fedora hat. His get-away car was driven by a woman dressed entirely in red. Their escape was thwarted by fire trucks. Their car was blocked by the trucks, and they were arrested by the police as they tried to run away from the scene of the crime.

_____

_____

_____

_____

_____

A Strong Beginning

Effective writing starts with the first word in the sentence. Avoid beginning your sentences with *there, it,* and *the.*

Example: **There** was an extra player in the backfield during that play.

Improved Sentence: During that play, an extra player was in the backfield.

■ Proofread each sentence in the paragraph, looking for weak beginnings. Revise each poor sentence. Recopy the improved paragraph.

Hints: You may need to use different words in your revised sentence.

Use action verbs to replace being verbs if possible.

Also, eliminate any unnecessary words.

Red and the Chewed Slipper

Edna sat on the sofa fuming. It happened again. There on the floor was her chewed slipper. There in the corner looking completely innocent was Red, the Irish setter. The dog was guilty, of course. Edna didn't need to take tooth prints to know that the dog had eaten the slipper, or most of it, for breakfast. "Oh, what am I ever to do with you?" sighed Edna. The sound of her voice stirred Red into action. It was his habit to walk over and nudge her gently when she was sad. And that is what he did.

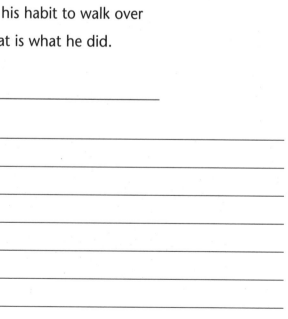

_____

_____

_____

_____

_____

_____

_____

_____

Expressing Feelings

Effective writing requires us to say what we mean in the most direct route. Of course, we must remember to use active voice and strong beginnings.

Example:

Puppy Love

I wasn't sure how Dad would react when I brought home a puppy. Dad always said, "I don't like pets." He took one look at my new puppy and said that I would have to care for and train the puppy. Dad surprised me, though, when I saw him scratching the puppy behind the ears one day. Then Dad began to take my puppy for walks. He fed the puppy treats. Soon, wherever you found Dad, you would find the puppy. Now Dad says, I still don't like pets, but I sure do love this puppy."

Write a paragraph about an event in your life. Express your feelings clearly about the situation. You may use one of the suggested topics.

Suggested Topics

The New Bike (Car, House, etc.)   My First Paycheck

The Day My Best Friend Moved   A Trip to ...

R
E
V
I
E
W

Review: Proofread, Revise, Recopy

Follow the directions.

- Proofread the paragraph.
- Revise the story.
- Recopy the improved paragraph.
- **Hints:** Replace passive voice with active voice.

   Replace weak beginning words with strong words.

   Get rid of extraneous sentences and unneeded words.

Moving Away, Again

The same house is stayed in by some people forever, it seems. That is not the case for us. We move once a year. Once we lived in a town called Springfield where I had a room to myself and lots of friends. I cried when we moved away. It was a miracle four years later when we moved back. I became best friends with a girl across the street. Such joy! That place was loved by me. I had a huge room of my own over the garage. Then, you guessed it, my dad was transferred again and away we went. Tears shed by me that time could have filled a reservoir.

Units 8–10 Test

A Identify each of the underlined phrases in the following sentences as similes, metaphors, or personification.

1. The <u>raindrops were drumsticks pounding</u> on my roof. _____

2. The <u>stars sparkled like diamonds</u> in the sky. _____

3. Jesse's <u>face was as worn as an old pair of sneakers</u>. _____

4. The <u>old car moaned and groaned as it limped</u> down the street. _____

5. Mariette's <u>answer was as certain as taxes</u>. _____

B Rewrite each of the following sentences, using active voice and a strong beginning. Provide a subject of your choice for sentences in which the doer of the action is not identified.

1. The bus was boarded by three people in Centerville.

_____

2. The dishes were washed, dried, and put away.

_____

3. The new soft drink was taste-tested by shoppers in the mall.

_____

4. Magazines are read and recycled by the students in my current events class.

_____

5. The package was carefully wrapped and mailed to my brother.

_____

C Write an expository paragraph about one of the following topics or a topic of your own choice. Remember to write a topic sentence and a summary or conclusion.

How to Make a Free-Throw Shot   The Worst Program on TV

_____
_____
_____
_____
_____
_____
_____
_____

The Narrative Paragraph

A **narrative paragraph** tells a story. A good story begins with an attention-catching sentence. For example, here is how Edgar Allan Poe's famous short story "The Tell-Tale Heart" begins:

True! Nervous—very nervous, dreadfully nervous I had been and am. But why will you say I am mad?

Ingredients of a Narrative	Conflict	a problem to be solved
	Plot	the events of the story
	Characters	heroes and villains pitted against each other
	Setting	the time and place of the story
	Theme	an idea the author wants to get across

Authors arrange the plot of a story so that the excitement builds. Near the end there is a decisive turning point. This is the **climax**. At the very end of the story there is a summing up; the author ties up the loose ends. This is called the **denouement**.

◼ Use the above information to complete each sentence.

1. A narrative paragraph tells a _____.

2. The story must have a problem to be solved called a _____.

3. The way the conflict is resolved makes up the _____.

4. The high point of the story (also called the turning point)
   is the _____.

5. The scene where the author ties up the loose ends is the _____.

6. The time and place of the story is the _____.

7. The idea the author tries to get across is the _____.

8. The people in a narrative are the _____.

Flashbacks

Writers sometimes use a technique called **flashback** to give the reader some background about a past event in the middle of the present action.

For example:

> Sharon sat down and remembered long ago when she and John Abbot were very young.
>
>   * * *
>
> John Abbot walked briskly into the room. He was wearing a silly smile.
>
> Sharon was puzzled. John was usually so serious. What could be the reason for his odd behavior?
>
> "I can't wait a second longer, " John said as he pulled a small box out of his jacket pocket and handed it to her.
>
>   * * *
>
> Smiling, Sharon looked at her left hand where the diamond ring that was in the box still sparkled as it had for more than twenty years.

Write a brief flashback that would explain the action in the following paragraph.

> Consuela's heart skipped a beat when she looked up and saw Eduardo Chavez enter the room. It had been more than thirty years since she'd last seen him, but she knew with certainty that it was he.

_____

_____

_____

_____

_____

_____

_____

_____

_____

_____

_____

_____

It Happened To Me: First Person Narrative

Personal pronouns have different forms for different persons depending on who is speaking:

First person: I looked slowly around the room and then announced, "I am leaving now."

Third person: He looked slowly around the room and then announced, "I am leaving now."

A writer can choose whether to tell a fictional story in the first person or in the third person. An autobiography would always be in the first person.

Rewrite the story below. Change it from the third person to the first person. Tell the story as if it happened to you. Use the pronoun *I* instead of *Heather* and *she.* Replace other pronouns and words as necessary. Do your work on a separate sheet of paper.

More than anything, Heather liked horseback riding. So, she was particularly happy that Saturday as her friend Maureen and she turned their horses onto a trail that led into the woods.

"Wait!" Maureen called out.

Heather turned Scout around and saw Maureen trying to stop her horse from nibbling the leaves from the trees hanging over the trail.

Heather trotted Scout back to help her friend. Suddenly, the horse realized it was headed toward the barn and took off at a fast trot. The reins were soon flapping in the wind, and Heather's feet came out of the stirrups. Scout's trot extended to a canter and then to a gallop. Seeing a fence directly in their path, Heather grabbed the mane tightly and shut her eyes. She felt herself lift into the air as Scout jumped the fence.

At last they reached the barnyard. Scout stopped and stood quietly by the fence as Heather dismounted. "What an incredible experience for an amateur rider!" she said. "I'll never forget this ride."

Direct Quotations

Dialogue is conversation. A **quotation** is the exact words someone says.

Rule 1: Put quotation marks at the beginning and end of a direct quotation.

"Help me! Help me!" Heather cried out.

Rule 2: Capitalize the first word in a quotation even when it is not the first word of the sentence.

Heather yelled, "My horse is running away."

Rule 3: You may identify the speaker at the beginning or end of the quotation. Use a comma when you name the speaker at the beginning.

Heather pleaded, "Please stop, Scout."

"Please stop, Scout!" pleaded Heather.

Rule 4: Usually enclose punctuation marks inside the closing quotation mark.

Maureen asked, "Are you all right, Heather?"

Rewrite the following story using only dialogue. Start a new paragraph each time you change speakers. The first sentence has been done as an example for you.

All week, Heather had been looking forward to going horseback riding with her friend Maureen. She had told Maureen what a good *equestrian* she was. An *equestrian* is a person who rides horses. Maureen was looking forward to riding also. She, however, had never ridden before. She hoped she would get a gentle horse. Heather wished for a spunky one that would give her a good ride.

Heather said to her friend Maureen, "All week, I have been looking forward to going horseback riding with you."

_____

_____

_____

_____

_____

_____

_____

_____

Indirect Quotations

Writers also use **indirect quotations** in narrative writing. An indirect quotation does not have quotation marks.

Direct: Heather begged, "Please help me with this horse!"

Indirect: Heather asked if she could get help with her horse.

A Change each of these direct quotations to an indirect quotation. Punctuate and capitalize correctly. Rewrite each sentence on the line.

1. "Not so fast. You're mixing me up," Costello said to Abbott.

   _____

2. The ball whizzed by, and the umpire hollered, "Strike three."

   _____

3. Jamal asked, "How soon will you be ready to leave?

   _____

4. "That coffee is too hot to drink," warned Annie.

   _____

5. "Well," sighed George, "you know I would help you if I could."

   _____

B Change each indirect quotation to a direct quotation. Punctuate and capitalize correctly. Rewrite each sentence on the line.

1. William told Claudia that he'd be home for dinner.

   _____

2. After the party, Jacune told April she had a good time.

   _____

3. I heard Miguel say that his car was in the shop.

   _____

4. I asked what had happened to my car.

   _____

5. Alice said that she would serve fruit for dessert.

   _____

Characterization

Characters are the people in a story. **Characterization** is the process of making persons in a story seem real. Outstanding characterizations in literature are

Scarlett O'Hara in *Gone With the Wind* by Margaret Mitchell.

Arthur Conan Doyle's Sherlock Holmes.

A Name some other fictional characters that you remember.

1. _____   3. _____

2. _____   4. _____

B Read the story. Then, follow the directions given.

Flossie

Flossie would rather have been anywhere but working in her sister Bessie's restaurant. Passers-by couldn't help but notice the tall, slender, dark-haired beauty sullenly tapping her foot to the music on the radio. Fortunately, it was nearly closing time. Since there hadn't been a customer in an hour, Flossie had half a mind to close up early. She chewed her gum impatiently and then blew a bubble.

Just then the doorbell jingled, and a thin, weedy-looking young man of about twenty-five walked through the door. He wore a gabardine overcoat with ragged sleeves and looked as though he was very hungry.

"Oh, darn!" she thought to herself. "Just the type to sit for an hour and end up buying only a cup of coffee. Hmm! It's awfully warm out for an overcoat."

As she scowled, her eyebrows turned in and then flew straight up. "Hand over all your money and make it quick," he said.

1. In your own words, write a short description of Flossie.

_____

_____

_____

2. Write a short description of the robber.

_____

_____

_____

Using Your Imagination: Dramatic License

Narration can be **fiction** or **nonfiction**. *Nonfiction* is a true story. *Fiction* is something you make up using your imagination. **Dramatic license** refers to the freedom to make up details to make your story better.

Flossie and the Robbery

Flossie's hand shook as she emptied the cash register and put the cash into a paper bag. Her fear, however, was not because of him, but rather because of what her sister Bessie would say when Flossie told her she'd given all her money away.

"There! That's all there is," she exclaimed.

He squinted as he looked into the bag. "Sure isn't much," he complained. A noise from a passing car startled him. "You lay down on the floor and don't get up for an hour. If anyone tries to follow me, he or she will be sorry."

Flossie knelt down thinking that she was going to get her new skirt dirty. "I would have cleaned this floor better, if I'd known," she thought. Then she heard the door shut.

"Good grief! Bessie's going to be furious," she thought as she leaped up and headed for the door.

■ Use you imagination to write answers for each item.

1. From what you know of Flossie, what do you think she will do next?

_____

_____

_____

_____

2. The writer has told you little about Flossie's sister, Bessie. Write a description of her. Tell how you think she might react when she hears about the robbery.

_____

_____

_____

_____

Review: Narrative Writing

 Read the following excerpt. Then finish the story. Write the scene between Flossie and Bessie (the denouement).

Woman Captures Robber

Flossie raced to the door. She caught a glimpse of the robber just turning the corner. Without stopping to think, she took off after him.

"Stop! Thief!" she yelled, but the people on the street only gazed at her. The only thought in Flossie's mind was that the robber had Bessie's money and that she had better get it back. She turned the corner and raced down the brick sidewalk. Then suddenly, there he was just ahead of her. Apparently, he had no idea that anyone would chase him.

"Stop!" she yelled again.

The robber turned his head, saw her, and took off running.

Flossie picked up speed herself, and then with one last all-out effort, she knocked him to the sidewalk just like a defensive end tackles a quarterback.

"OK, OK, lady. Take your money." He threw the paper bag at her.

She held him down anyway until a police officer arrived.

"I'll take over now," the officer said as she handcuffed the suspect.

Relieved, Flossie released the suspect.

The officer thanked her and said that she deserved a citizen's award for her action. The officer cautioned Flossie, however, to call the police immediately the next time something happened at the restaurant.

_____

_____

_____

_____

_____

_____

_____

_____

_____

_____

_____

Persuasive Writing

Sometimes we write to inform; sometimes we write to persuade. The most common type of **persuasive writing** is advertisements. Television commercials have a strong influence on what people buy and what they think. They choose words that we will respond to.

Examples: new   fresh   natural   bigger   improved

A Make a list of words that deliver a positive message. Look at advertisements in magazines and newspapers for ideas.

1. _____
2. _____
3. _____
4. _____
5. _____

6. _____
7. _____
8. _____
9. _____
10. _____

11. _____
12. _____
13. _____
14. _____
15. _____

B Look over the list of words below. Circle the ones that are most appealing to you. Think about the reasons why they are appealing.

awesome	heavy	lazy	delightful
gaudy	velvety	tart	economical
precious	angry	courageous	cheap
changing	cautious	organized	clueless

C Think about some popular advertisements on television. Describe one ad you like. Explain what you like about it.

_____

_____

_____

_____

_____

_____

_____

_____

Slogans

A **slogan** is a brief attention-getting statement that we use to advertise a product.

Examples: Good to the last drop

The real thing

Reach out and touch someone

A Write a slogan for each kind of product listed. Use the name of a product you know or make up a name for the product.

1. laundry soap _____

_____

2. peanut butter _____

_____

3. dog food _____

_____

4. a computer _____

_____

5. frozen pizza _____

_____

B Select one of the products above and write a longer description designed to persuade someone to buy it.

_____

_____

_____

_____

_____

_____

_____

_____

_____

Using Facts to Persuade

Along with appealing words, you can also use information to effectively persuade another person. To persuade people to move to your town or city, you might tell them some advantages.

Examples: parks   skating rink   recreational activities   schools

A Make a list of information about the town or city where you live. Write all the positive things you can think of. Be very specific. You can write to the Bureau of the Census for factual information.

_____

_____

_____

_____

_____

_____

_____

B Now, use the information you have listed to design an advertising campaign to promote your town or city. Write a short speech to persuade people to move to your town. Make up a snappy slogan.

Slogan: _____

_____

_____

_____

_____

_____

_____

_____

_____

_____

Read the letter to the editor of a newspaper. The letter contains information about an issue that the person wanted others to know about.

June 12, 1997

Dear Editor:

This city needs additional parks. Years ago when the original developers planned the town, they set aside a large recreational area for each neighborhood. Since that time, people have built houses here and there on nearly every vacant lot. The number of people has doubled, but not one new park has been established. Before we fill every speck of land with groups of houses and apartments, let's stop and think. Where will the children play? Where will the families picnic? Which is more important, the city tax base or our quality of life?

Sincerely yours,

Jocelyn Corelli

Think about an issue in your town or city. Write a letter to the editor. Use a separate sheet of paper to write your rough draft. Write the final copy on the lines below.

Dear Editor:

_____

_____

_____

_____

_____

_____

_____

_____

_____

Review: Persuasive Writing

 Select one of the following topics. Write a short speech to persuade someone about your topic. Use a separate sheet of paper to write your rough draft. Write the final copy on the lines provided.

Hints: Start with an attention-getting topic sentence.

Use facts and details to convince your readers.

Pay attention to sentence structure and correct usage.

Remember that spelling always counts.

Topics: Never Drink and Drive

Eat a Balanced Diet

A High School Diploma Is Important to Your Future

Every Citizen Should Vote in All Elections

_____

_____

_____

_____

_____

_____

_____

_____

_____

_____

_____

_____

_____

The Letter Format

Letters can be formal or informal; however, they all have a basic format.

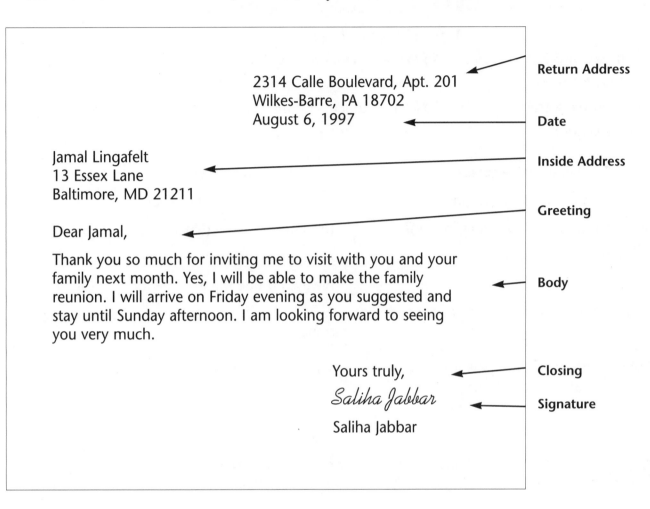

2314 Calle Boulevard, Apt. 201
Wilkes-Barre, PA 18702 ← Return Address
August 6, 1997 ← Date

Jamal Lingafelt ← Inside Address
13 Essex Lane
Baltimore, MD 21211

Greeting

Dear Jamal,

Thank you so much for inviting me to visit with you and your
family next month. Yes, I will be able to make the family
reunion. I will arrive on Friday evening as you suggested and ← Body
stay until Sunday afternoon. I am looking forward to seeing
you very much.

Yours truly, ← Closing
Saliha Jabbar ← Signature
Saliha Jabbar

Identify each part of a letter. Write the letter on the line.

_____ **1.** Signature   **a.** Dear Jamal,

_____ **2.** Greeting   **b.** Saliha Jabbar

_____ **3.** Closing   **c.** The sender's address

_____ **4.** Return address   **d.** The recipient's address

_____ **5.** Inside address   **e.** Yours truly,

_____ **6.** Body   **f.** The contents of the letter

Personal Letters

A **personal letter** is also called a *friendly* letter or an *informal* letter. It is a letter to someone you know on a personal basis; for example, a friend or relative.

Types of Personal Letters

Bread and Butter note:	To express thanks for a visit to someone's home
Thank You note:	To thank someone for a gift or a kind act
Personal letter:	To keep in touch with friends and family
Invitation:	To invite someone to a party or an event

Personal Letters	Formal Letters
Insert a comma after the greeting.	Insert a colon after the greeting.
Use a friendly close (Love, Your friend,).	Use a formal close (Sincerely,).
Inside address is optional.	Always include an inside address.
The return address is optional.	Always include the return address.
Your typed or printed name is not needed.	Always include your full name as well as your signature.
A friendly letter may be typewritten, but it is more personal if handwritten.	A business letter should be typewritten.

Write a sample bread and butter note of your own. Write about the last time you visited someone's home. Use your best handwriting.

_____

_____

_____

_____

_____

_____

_____

_____

_____

Business Letters

A **business letter** is a formal letter. One business letter many people write is a letter to their high school principal asking that their school transcripts be sent to a college or an employer. When you write this kind of business letter, always mention your full legal name and the dates you attended the school or the date you graduated.

Use the space below to write a letter to your school principal. Ask your principal to send your transcript to the college of your choice.

Hint: Find the addresses of local colleges in a telephone book. Addresses of colleges and universities may also be listed in a dictionary and an almanac.

Your name _____

Your address _____

City, state, ZIP code _____

Today's date _____

_____ Principal's name

_____ Name of school

_____ Street address

_____ City, state, ZIP code

_____ Greeting

_____
_____
_____
_____
_____ Body
_____
_____
_____

Closing _____

Signature _____

Name _____

Addressing Envelopes

U N I T 13

Of course, your letter will never reach its destination unless you address the envelope correctly.

Saliha Jabbar
2314 Calle Boulevard, Apt. 201
Wilkes-Barre, PA 18702

Jamal Lingafelt
13 Essex Lane
Baltimore, MD 21211

A Address this envelope to yourself. Include your name on the first line, your street address and apartment number, if applicable, on the second line, and your city, state, and ZIP code on the third line.

Saliha Jabbar
2314 Calle Boulevard, Apt. 201
Wilkes-Barre, PA 18702

B You should always include a return address on your envelope. The return address should be placed in the upper, left corner of an envelope. The return address enables the postal service to return a letter that cannot be delivered. Write your return address on this envelope.

Saliha Jabbar
2314 Calle Boulevard, Apt. 201
Wilkes-Barre, PA 18702

Review: Letter Writing

Write a formal letter to a teacher, friend, or business. Ask the person you write to provide you with a job recommendation. Do your rough draft on a separate sheet of paper. Write your final copy in the following space.

Check List: Did you include your return address, today's date, the inside address, a greeting (with a colon after the name), one or more solid paragraphs in the body, a closing, your signature, your printed name? Are you sure all the words are spelled correctly? Check for sentence structure.

Units 11–13 Test

A Change the following quotations to indirect quotations.

1. Benjamin Franklin wrote, "Necessity never made a good bargain."

_____

2. "Lost time is never found," wrote Benjamin Franklin.

_____

3. In *The American Crisis,* Thomas Paine wrote, "These are the times that try men's souls."

_____

B Read the following letter and answer the questions about it.

8001 Colt Drive
Boise, Idaho 83709
December 12, 1996

Ms. Rebecca Angelise
Vice-President of Manufacturing
Coltran Corporation
1817 North 74th Street
Elmwood Park, IL 60035

Dear Ms. Angelise:

Recently, I purchased a birdhouse manufactured by your company. After just two months, the roof of the house separated from the rest of it. Enclosed is my receipt for the purchase of the house. Since the house came with a warranty, I am requesting a replacement house for the defective one or a refund of the purchase price. I would appreciate your immediate attention to this matter.

Sincerely,
Maura Fairbanks
Maura Fairbanks

---

1. When was the letter written? _____

2. What is the greeting of the letter? _____

3. What is the closing of the letter? _____

4. Who wrote the letter? _____

5. Where does the writer live? _____

6. Is the letter a business or a friendly letter? _____

7. To whom was the letter written? _____

End-of-Book Test

A In the blank, write the letter of the answer that best completes each statement.

_____ 1. Two words that are examples of homophones are

    a. wet/dry.   **b.** quick/fast.
    c. herd/heard.   **d.** there/fair.

_____ 2. The plural of the word *battery* is spelled

    a. batterys.   **b.** batteries.
    c. batteris.   **d.** batteres.

_____ 3. A word that has a meaning similar to *affect* is

    a. influence.   **b.** effect.
    c. emit.   **d.** result.

_____ 4. The past tense of the verb *swim* is

    a. swim.   **b.** swimmed.
    c. swimed.   **d.** swam.

_____ 5. The word *forget* plus the suffix *-able* is spelled

    a. forgetable.   **b.** forgettable.
    c. forgetible.   **d.** forgotable.

_____ 6. "Happy as a lark" is an example of

    a. a metaphor.   **b.** personification.
    c. a simile.   **d.** an adjective.

B Rewrite each of these sentences, adding punctuation where needed.

1. Who is at the door

_____

2. The clown was wearing a purple tutu a polka dot vest and an orange shirt

_____

3. Ms. Jarvis read a list of words and we wrote the list on our papers

_____

4. What a fantastic show that was

_____

5. Will Jamal and Latina be joining us

_____

6. If we are going to be on time we have to leave now.

_____

C Circle the word in parentheses that best completes each sentence.

1. Carlos and Raul are twins, and I often get (they, them, their) mixed up.

2. Malory and (I, me, mine) take the same train every day.

3. Have you seen the (student, students', students) new computer room.

4. We saw (whales, whale's, whales') off the coast of Massachusetts.

5. *A Tale of Two Cities* begins, "It was the (goodest, better, best) of times, it was the worst of times."

6. The lobster scene was the (funny, funnier, funniest) scene in the entire movie.

7. The building is even (beautifuler, more beautiful, most beautiful) since it has been renovated.

8. The varsity played yesterday and so (do, did, done) the freshman team.

9. I (was, could have been, had been) here earlier if I had not missed the bus.

10. He is leaving for Texas on July 1, but she (has been, is being, was) there since June 5.

D In the paragraph, label the topic sentence, circle the summary statement, and cross out any extraneous sentences.

Dolly Parton is a woman with many talents. She is an award-winning singer and song writer. Among her biggest hits are "Jolene" and "I Will Always Love You." Whitney Houston sang "I Will Always Love You" in the movie *The Bodyguard.* Parton is also a motion picture actor, who had starring roles in the movies *Nine to Five* and *Steel Magnolias.* Parton opened her own theme park in Tennessee, and she is the owner of music publishing and film production companies. Parton was born in Tennessee in 1946. Parton truly is a most gifted individual.

E On a separate sheet of paper, write a narrative paragraph, persuasive paragraph, or a business letter. Remember to avoid run-on sentences and sentence fragments.